PROTAGORAS

PLATO (*c*.427–347 BC), Athenian philosopher-dramatist, has had a profound and lasting influence upon Western intellectual tradition. Born into a wealthy and prominent family, he grew up during the conflict between Athens and the Peloponnesian states which engulfed the Greek world from 431 to 404 BC. Following its turbulent aftermath, he was deeply affected by the condemnation and execution of his revered master Socrates (469–399) on charges of irreligion and corrupting the young. In revulsion from political activity, Plato devoted his life to the pursuit of philosophy and to composing memoirs of Socratic inquiry cast in dialogue form. He was strongly influenced by the Pythagorean thinkers of southern Italy and Sicily, which he is said to have visited when he was about 40. Some time after returning to Athens, he founded the Academy, an early ancestor of the modern university, devoted to philosophical and mathematical inquiry, and to the education of future rulers or 'philosopher kings'. The Academy's most celebrated member was the young Aristotle (384–322), who studied there for the last twenty years of Plato's life.

Plato is the earliest Western philosopher from whose output complete works have been preserved. At least twenty-five of his dialogues are extant, ranging from fewer than twenty to more than three hundred pages in length. For their combination of dramatic realism, poetic beauty, intellectual vitality, and emotional power they are unique in Western literature.

C. C. W. TAYLOR is Emeritus Professor of Philosophy, Oxford University, and an Emeritus Fellow of Corpus Christi College. His publications include *Plato, Protagoras* (Clarendon Plato Series, 2nd edn. 1991), *The Greeks on Pleasure* (with J. C. B. Gosling) (Clarendon Press, 1982), *Socrates* (OUP, 1998), *The Atomists: Leucippus and Democritus, Fragments*, a text and translation with a commentary (Toronto UP, 1999), *Aristotle, Nicomachean Ethics II–IV* (Clarendon Aristotle Series, 2006) and *Pleasure, Mind, and Soul, Selected Papers* (Clarendon Press, 2008).

OXFORD WORLD'S CLASSICS

For over 100 years Oxford World's Classics have brought
readers closer to the world's great literature. Now with over 700
titles—from the 4,000-year-old myths of Mesopotamia to the
twentieth century's greatest novels—the series makes available
lesser-known as well as celebrated writing.

The pocket-sized hardbacks of the early years contained
introductions by Virginia Woolf, T. S. Eliot, Graham Greene,
and other literary figures which enriched the experience of reading.
Today the series is recognized for its fine scholarship and
reliability in texts that span world literature, drama and poetry,
religion, philosophy and politics. Each edition includes perceptive
commentary and essential background information to meet the
changing needs of readers.

OXFORD WORLD'S CLASSICS

PLATO

Protagoras

Translated with an Introduction and Notes by
C. C. W. TAYLOR

OXFORD
UNIVERSITY PRESS

OXFORD
UNIVERSITY PRESS

Great Clarendon Street, Oxford OX2 6DP

Oxford University Press is a department of the University of Oxford.
It furthers the University's objective of excellence in research, scholarship,
and education by publishing worldwide in

Oxford New York

Auckland Bangkok Buenos Aires Cape Town Chennai
Dar es Salaam Delhi Hong Kong Istanbul Karachi Kolkata
Kuala Lumpur Madrid Melbourne Mexico City Mumbai Nairobi
São Paulo Shanghai Singapore Taipei Tokyo Toronto

with an associated company in Berlin

Oxford is a registered trade mark of Oxford University Press
in the UK and in certain other countries

Published in the United States
by Oxford University Press Inc., New York

© C. C. W. Taylor 1996

The moral rights of the author have been asserted
Database right Oxford University Press (maker)

First published as a World's Classics paperback 1996
Reissued as an Oxford World's Classics paperback 2002
Reissued 2009

British Library Cataloguing in Publication Data

Data available

Library of Congress Cataloging in Publication Data

Plato
[Protagoras, English]
Protagoras / Plato; translated by C. C. W. Taylor.
p. cm.—(Oxford world's classics)
Includes bibliographical references and index.
1. Protagoras. 2. Socrates. 3. Sophists (Greek philosophy).
4. Ethics. I. Taylor, C. C. W. (Christopher Charles Whiston),
1926– . II. Title. III. Series
B382.A5T39 1996 170—dc20 96–7901

ISBN 978–0–19–955565–9

Printed in Great Britain by
Clays Ltd, Elcograf S.p.A.

CONTENTS

ABBREVIATIONS

Ancient Authors

Ar.	Aristotle
EN	*Nicomachean Ethics*
Met.	*Metaphysics*
Pol.	*Politics*
Arist.	Aristophanes
D.L.	Diogenes Laertius
Hdt.	Herodotus
	Homer
Od.	*Odyssey*
	Plato
Alc. I & II	*Alcibiades I & II*
Apol.	*Apology*
Charm.	*Charmides*
Crit.	*Critias*
Ep.	*Letters*
Euthyd.	*Euthydemus*
Gorg.	*Gorgias*
Hipp. Maj.	*Greater Hippias*
Hipp. Min.	*Lesser Hippias*
Lach.	*Laches*
Ph.	*Phaedo*
Phaedr.	*Phaedrus*
Pol.	*Politicus (Statesman)*
Prot.	*Protagoras*
Rep.	*Republic*
Soph.	*Sophist*
Symp.	*Symposium*
Tht.	*Theaetetus*
Tim.	*Timaeus*
Plut.	Plutarch
Alc.	*Life of Alcibiades*
Xen.	Xenophon
Mem.	*Memorabilia (Memoirs) of Socrates*
Symp.	*Symposium*

ABBREVIATIONS

Modern Works

AP	*Ancient Philosophy*
DK	H. Diels and W. Kranz, *Die Fragmente der Vorsokratiker*, 6th and subsequent edns., Berlin, 1952–
JHP	*Journal of the History of Philosophy*
OSAP	*Oxford Studies in Ancient Philosophy*
PR	*Philosophical Review*
RM	*Review of Metaphysics*
SM	G. B. Kerferd, *The Sophistic Movement*, Cambridge, 1981

INTRODUCTION

IN the *Protagoras* Plato represents, with the highest degree of dramatic artistry, a discussion between Socrates and the leading sophists of his day on a fundamental moral question, how can one acquire the ability to live the best possible life. In this introduction I shall attempt to explore the interwoven themes of sophistry, the portrayal of Socrates, and the significance of the question which he debates with the sophists. That exploration will also, I hope, throw some light on why the dialogue takes the particular shape, and treats the particular topics it does.

For our purpose Socrates and the sophists are two sides of a single coin, in that the contrast between the two is one of the most important aspects of Plato's portrayal of Socrates. As pointed out in the Explanatory Note on 312a, the sophists were regarded in some quarters as dangerous subversives who taught young men to overthrow established moral conventions with logic-chopping arguments, and there is every reason to believe that Socrates, whose characteristic method of argument had in fact much in common with sophistic methods, was tarred (in some people's minds) with the same brush. Plato certainly believed, very probably rightly, that that association had been instrumental in creating the climate of opinion which had led to the condemnation and death of Socrates (that is one of the main themes of his *Apology*). It was therefore central to his portrayal of Socrates as the ideal philosopher and educator to represent his activity as antithetical to that of the sophists. So far from its being the case that Socrates was (as popularly perceived) a home-grown, unpaid sophist, Socrates is the genuine exemplar of the philosophical life, of which the sophists merely peddle a counterfeit.

The so-called 'Sophistic Movement' was a complex phenomenon. In the fifth century BC the increasing intellectual sophistication, economic prosperity, and political development of a number of Greek states, particularly Athens,

ix

created a demand for education going beyond the traditional elementary grounding in music and literature (especially poetry), arithmetic, and physical training (see Explanatory Note on 312b). To a certain extent this took the form of the popularization of the tradition of speculation about the physical world instituted by the Ionian philosophers of the sixth century, which was extended into areas such as history, geography, and the origins of civilization. (Protagoras' story of Prometheus in the dialogue is an example of the latter kind of discussion.) The demand for success in forensic and political oratory, fostered by the increase in participatory democracy which was a feature of political life, especially in Athens, led to the development of specialized techniques of persuasion and argument, associated in particular with the names of Gorgias and Protagoras. Finally, the sophists were associated with a rationalistic and critical attitude to things in general, with implications, unwelcome to those of conservative views, for matters of morality and religion. The satisfaction of this complex of demands gave rise to a new profession, that of itinerant teachers who travelled the Greek world lecturing and giving other kinds of instruction to those who were prepared to pay. It was essentially an individualistic activity, an extension to new areas of the older tradition of the itinerant rhapsode (i.e. reciter of poems). The sophists belonged to no organization, nor did they share a common body of belief, and they founded no schools, either in the sense of academic institutions or in that of groups of individuals committed to the promulgation of specific philosophical doctrines.

None of these aspects of the sophists' activity was without some impact on Socrates, according to Plato's portrayal of him. According to the account of his intellectual development given in the *Phaedo* (96a–99d), he was at one time deeply interested in physical speculation, though he appears to have abandoned it in favour of concentration on ethical questions. But he was not thereby led to a mechanistic outlook. That is not to say that his approach to the physical world was not rationalistic; rather, his rationalism led him to reject mechanistic explanations as inadequate, since they could provide no account of the reasons for which things happened. For that it was necessary to show how things happened as a rational agent would arrange them, i.e. for the best. That same rationalistic assumption is at the heart of Plato's version of Socratic morality. Every rational agent is uniformly motivated to seek what is best, understood in self-interested terms as what is best for the agent; given that constant motivation, understanding of what is in fact for the best is sufficient to guarantee conduct designed to achieve it. But rather than leading to the abandonment of conventional morality, as in the case of opponents such as Thrasymachus and Callicles whom Plato represents as arguing against Socrates, this rationalism presents Plato's Socrates with the task of showing that adherence to the traditional virtues of courage, self-control, etc. is in fact beneficial to the agent. In so doing Socrates rejects the antithesis, widely accepted by adherents of the sophists, between *nomos*, law or convention (including morality) and *phusis*, nature (see Explanatory Note on 337d); so far from conflicting with the promptings of nature, as alleged e.g. by Antiphon, morality is necessary for humans to achieve what nature (i.e. rational organization) has designed them to seek, namely, what is best for them. As regards techniques of argument, Socrates indeed relied on a technique which was one of those pioneered by the sophists, that of subjection of a hypothesis, proposed by a participant in debate, to critical questioning, with a view to eliciting a contradiction in the set of beliefs held by the proponent of the hypothesis. In this case the difference was not in method, but in aim. Plato consistently represents the sophists as treating argument as a competitive game (see Explanatory Note on 335a) in which victory was achieved by reducing one's opponent to self-contradiction, whereas Socrates regarded argument as a co-operative enterprise in which the participants are not opponents but partners in the search for truth (360e–361a). Reduction of one's interlocutor to self-contradiction is not the end of the game, as it is for the sophists, but a necessary stage on the path of discovery (see *Meno* 84a–d).

One of Plato's main purposes in writing was to defend the

memory of Socrates by presenting him as the ideal philosopher, and we have seen how that project requires that he be distanced from the sophists with whom he had been, superficially but none the less disastrously, associated. The *Protagoras* exemplifies this programme throughout. It begins by contrasting the uncritical enthusiasm of the young Hippocrates for sophistic teaching with Socrates' principled concern for what is of fundamental importance, the effect of that teaching on the soul. Protagoras claims as a distinctive merit of his own teaching its concentration on the question of how to become an outstanding individual (318d–319a), but he proves to have no coherent conception of the nature of human excellence, and presents himself as merely complementing, rather than offering any genuine alternative to, the unsystematic transmission of moral tradition which constitutes conventional education. Here as elsewhere (e.g. *Republic* 492–3) Plato stresses the paradox that, while the sophists were feared as dangerous radicals, much of their teaching was deeply conservative, relying ultimately on accepted opinions. Socrates, by contrast, calls for a radical re-examination of the foundations of that popular morality, which may require abandonment of traditional beliefs, e.g. that justice involves doing good to one's friends and harm to one's enemies (*Republic* 334b–335d). Any such reshaping of traditional belief takes place within a framework of adherence to the traditional virtues, but the conception of what these virtues are is open to adjustment in the light of Socrates' psychological theory; thus in the concluding section of the *Protagoras* Socrates defends, on the basis of a hedonistic version of his theory of self-interested motivation, a revisionary account of courage as knowledge of the good and harm, i.e. pleasure and pain, expected to be brought about by one's actions. (On Socrates' attitude towards this hedonistic assumption, see below.)

In the foregoing remarks I have emphasized the apologetic character of Plato's portrayal of Socrates, putting particular stress on one aspect of that portrayal which is specially relevant to the *Protagoras*, the contrast between the figure of

Socrates, the ideal philosopher, and those of his fraudulent rivals, the sophists. It is important to realize that Plato's portrayal is a literary creation with its own particular aims, and thus to steer a middle course between two erroneous assumptions which, though incompatible with one another, are liable to seem equally obvious and attractive to the inexperienced reader. These are the assumptions that the Socratic dialogues are on the one hand historical records of actual conversations, and on the other expositions of Plato's philosophical doctrines. In fact, Plato's Socratic dialogues are a contribution to an established literary genre; at least nine of Socrates' associates are reported as having written depictions of his conversations, and the genre was sufficiently well established for Aristotle to mention it incidentally in his *Poetics* ($1447^{b}9-13$) as belonging to the same 'poetic' type as the mimes of Sophron and Xenarchus, dramatic representations of scenes from ordinary life.[1] As is obvious from comparison between the Socratic writings of Plato and Xenophon, each writer presented Socrates in accordance with his own particular interests; Xenophon is quite explicit about his apologetic agenda at the beginning of his *Memorabilia*, and carries it out by presenting conversations in which Socrates is characterized primarily by commitment to conventional morality and to the good of others. While these conversations are not entirely devoid of philosophical content, that element is much less prominent than in Plato's dialogues. Xenophon sometimes claims to be reporting conversations at which he was present, but that may itself be a mere literary device.[2] Plato never makes that claim in his own person; most of the dialogues depict conversations at which he could not have been present (including the *Protagoras*, whose dramatic date is about six years before he was born), and could, therefore,

---

[1] See D. Clay, 'The Origins of the Socratic Dialogue', in P. A. Vander Waerdt (ed.), *The Socratic Movement* (Ithaca, NY, Cornell University Press, 1994), 23–47.

[2] R. Waterfield points out (*Xenophon, Conversations of Socrates* (Harmondsworth, Penguin Books, 1990), introd., p. 21) that Xenophon claims to have been present at the dinner-party depicted in his *Symposium*, which took place at a dramatic date at which he was still a child.

present a historical record only on the assumption that some participant gave Plato a verbatim report, in some cases twenty or more years later. This is not to say that Plato's dialogues are total fictions; most of the characters are real persons, and it is plausible to suppose that their personalities are depicted with reasonable fidelity. Some of the dialogues (including the *Protagoras*) may, for all we know, be based on reports of actual conversations. What is crucial is that, for Plato's apologetic and philosophical purposes, historical truth is largely irrelevant; to take this dialogue as an example, the significance of the confrontation between Socrates and the sophists is entirely independent of the questions whether Socrates ever met Protagoras at the house of Callias, or whether, if he did, the conversation took anything like the course depicted in the dialogue.

It would betray an equal misunderstanding of Plato's purposes in writing to suppose that the dialogues are intended as straightforward expositions of Plato's own doctrines. It is important to emphasize 'straightforward', since I should not wish to follow some radical commentators[3] in denying that the dialogues have any expository element. Plato believed that the aim of philosophy is to achieve a reasoned grasp of the truth, and that the paradigm method of so doing is the oral interchange exemplified by Socratic question and answer. Only by actively engaging with a philosophical position in argument can one achieve genuine critical understanding. The written word, whose author is not available for critical examination, is not the appropriate medium for the imparting of that understanding (see Explanatory Note on 347c–e); hence there can be no exposition of Plato's philosophy in a written treatise (*Seventh Letter* 341c).[4] It follows that Plato's primary aim in writing was not to teach Platonic philosophy, since teaching philosophy is teaching people to philosophize, and that is not something which one can do by

[3] e.g. M. C. Stokes, *Plato's Socratic Conversations* (London, Athlone Press, 1986).

[4] The authenticity of the Platonic letters is disputed, but it is generally agreed that, even if the Seventh Letter was not written by Plato, it is an authentic statement of Platonic doctrine.

writing. Whether Plato had a single primary aim throughout his literary career seems to me highly doubtful. As far as the *Protagoras* is concerned, I think that his primary aim was to present the confrontation between Socrates and the sophists which I have described above. Subsidiary to that, I think that he attempts, by drawing the reader into a living argument, to encourage him to engage for him or herself in the exploration of human excellence and the way in which it can be acquired. Among the arguments presented are some which Plato probably recognized as unsound (see Explanatory Note on 329d–331b), which are included purely to stimulate the reader's critical faculties, and some (especially in the final section) which he held to be sound. Yet even there Plato's aim is not to convince his readers by the force of the written word, but to encourage them to establish the conclusion for themselves via their own critical reasoning.[5]

The question of how excellence is to be acquired (which is also the starting-point of the *Meno*, a dialogue probably written shortly after the *Protagoras*), is ideally suited to focus the contrast between Socrates and the sophists. Since the latter purported to supersede traditional forms of education, it immediately raises the question of the distinctiveness of what they had to offer, and its relation to tradition. In both *Protagoras* and *Meno* it becomes clear that an adequate answer presupposes an understanding of what excellence is, the question which reveals the distinctiveness of Socrates' moral psychology and thereby the basic divergence between his view and that of Protagoras. In the *Meno* that presupposition is explicitly argued for at the outset of the discussion (71b). In the *Protagoras* it emerges implicitly as the discussion unfolds. Challenged by Socrates to make good his claim to teach excellence, Protagoras responds by telling the story of Prometheus, which contains an account of human excellence as the basic social virtues of justice and self-control. On this account human excellence is nothing more than moral virtue, and moral virtue is that sense of fairness, respect for

---

[5] For fuller discussion see Taylor, *Protagoras* comm., introd. pp. xvi–xvii.

others, and self-restraint which is required of everyone if human society is to function in a hostile world. But while Protagoras gives a clear and convincing account of the social mechanisms by which that basic social morality is inculcated, he has tacitly shifted the terms of the question from Hippocrates' initial concern 'How can I become a leading figure in the state?' and in so doing has left it quite obscure how the sophist can make any distinctive contribution to the acquisition of excellence. There is thus an incoherence in Protagoras' defence, which stems from his failure to articulate a satisfactory account of what excellence is. The question of the unity of the virtues (see below) to which the rest of the dialogue is mainly devoted, is in fact the search for such an account. Socrates seeks first to establish that Protagoras' picture of excellence as a cluster of distinct virtues is incoherent; as suggested above, I doubt whether Plato regarded these arguments as satisfactory. After the discussion of the poem of Simonides (see below), the discussion is renewed, focusing on the case of courage. After another, probably deliberately abortive, dialectical exercise (349e–350c), in the final section Socrates argues from what Plato, in my (controversial) view, regards as true principles of moral psychology (including the identification of the good with an overall pleasant life) that courage (and by implication each of the specific virtues) is identical with knowledge of the good.

The discussion of the poem is one of the most puzzling parts of the dialogue for the modern reader; why should Plato devote so much space (almost one-seventh of the whole dialogue) and assign such a central position to discussion of a topic which is prima facie incidental to its main theme, a discussion, moreover, which is transparently non-serious, not to say frivolous? Hence philosophically minded commentators tend either to ignore this passage altogether or to refer to it with some embarrassment as an 'interlude', to be hurried over as briefly as possible before returning to the serious business of the dialogue, the arguments on the unity of the virtues. The supposedly incidental character of the subject must be distinguished from the alleged frivolity of its treatment. The former is illusory; the central topic of the dialogue is moral education, including the claim of the sophists to provide it, and the elucidation of the poets was, as Protagoras says (338e–339a), an important element in the sophists' curriculum. In turning to the elucidation of a poem Plato is indeed diverting from his immediate topic, the nature of excellence; but this detour leads the reader back to a central question of the dialogue, namely, 'How can a sophist teach excellence?' Protagoras has already given one example of the method and content of his teaching in the story of Prometheus and its elucidation; that is now to be supplemented by an example of another method, criticism of a poem on a moral theme. The question of frivolity is more complicated. The treatment of the poem is in a way frivolous (see below), but the frivolity itself has a serious purpose, that of out-sophisting the sophists and thereby demonstrating the essential frivolity of their undertaking to make criticism of poetry a staple of moral education.

Protagoras' approach to the poem is eristic; he treats the poet as an antagonist in the argumentative game, to be defeated by being shown to contradict himself; his victory is marked by a shout of applause from the audience (339d). Socrates in response takes on the role of verbal pugilist; Protagoras has nearly knocked him out, so he hangs on and goes in for some shady tactics to give him time to recover his senses (339e). This episode, in which Prodicus, who is explicitly said to be joking (341d7), sides with Socrates against his professional rival, is treated as a prelude to what purports to be Socrates' real elucidation of the poem (342a ff.). This continues the theme of eristic. Protagoras, who had claimed the poets as forerunners of the sophistic tradition (316d), treats a poet as an object for eristic attack; Socrates, in his role as an argumentative combatant, goes one better by representing the poet himself as a practitioner of eristic against one of the renowned Wise Men of the past. The sophistic tradition, then, is as a whole eristic, in contrast with the genuine philosophical tradition of the Sages, which has its roots in, of all unlikely places, Sparta and Crete. The detailed exposition of Simonides' refutation of Pittacus 'reveals' the poet as a Socratic, maintaining among other things that the only misfortune is to be deprived of knowledge and that no one does wrong willingly. All this is set out in a long speech which balances those which Protagoras had previously delivered, and exemplifies the method which Socrates has already contrasted unfavourably with that of question and answer. The lesson, that this method, given the eristic aim of the whole activity, can be used to force any arbitrary interpretation on a text, is explicitly spelled out at 347e.

The critique of sophistic interpretation implied in Socrates' parody thus contains a number of interconnected strands: (*a*) in this activity sophists aim at eristic triumph rather than truth; (*b*) the method of long speeches characteristically employed in this activity is a less disciplined method than that of question and answer; (*c*) it is not possible to establish with certainty any interpretation of a written text, since it is impossible to elicit knowledge of authors' intentions by questioning them. Taken together they constitute a serious critique of sophistic method, a critique which is not invalidated by the irresponsibility with which Socrates forces Simonides' thought into a Socratic mould (indeed the irresponsibility, being an exemplar of what is criticized, is essential to the critique). We must, however, recall that, since we have no surviving examples of actual sophistic poetic interpretation, we cannot judge the fairness or otherwise of Socrates' criticisms. Obviously, even if sophists typically sought argumentative victory rather than truth, it was not necessary that they should do so. Again, even if the sophists were to concede that it is impossible to establish the truth of any interpretation with certainty (a thesis which is itself not beyond dispute), they might have contented themselves with the claim that some could be established with sufficient plausibility to make it worthwhile to consider whether what the author says is true, and might have supported that by pointing out that Plato's own practice in writing presupposes the truth of that more modest thesis. Again, as Protagoras' actual example (339b–d) shows, criticism of poetry can be as well conducted by question and answer as by long speeches. In short, while Socrates has raised some serious questions about the status of this aspect of sophistic education, it cannot be claimed that he has succeeded in showing that it is worthless.

The main substantive topic of the dialogue, that of the nature of excellence, has attracted a great deal of scholarly discussion, largely because of the difficulty of determining precisely what thesis it is which Socrates is represented as urging against Protagoras. As far as Protagoras is concerned, it is clear that he takes a view of the specific virtues, courage, self-control, etc., which is broadly that of ordinary Greek opinion, namely, that they are distinct attributes in the way that e.g. the different bodily senses are distinct. A properly functioning human being must possess them all (in good working order), but each has its own intrinsic nature, and it is possible to have some while lacking others. Under pressure from Socrates he is prepared to concede that the virtues other than courage 'resemble one another fairly closely', but he holds out for the view that courage is completely different from the rest, since people who are grossly deficient in respect of the others can nevertheless be outstandingly courageous (349d). On the identification of Socrates' position agreement has been more elusive. One influential view is that of Vlastos, in 'The Unity of the Virtues in the *Protagoras*'; he holds that what the Socratic thesis comes to is that whoever possesses any one of the specific excellences necessarily possesses all the others, since the possession of any specific excellence requires that its possessor should have a firm grasp of what is best for the individual, which is in turn sufficient for the possession of all the specific excellences. Thus someone who knows what is best for humans will know that the attainment of it requires justice, holiness, etc., and someone who has that knowledge is thereby guaranteed to behave in the appropriate ways. This interpretation requires that sentences such as 'Justice is the same thing as holiness' should be understood in a special, technical sense (for details see Vlastos, 'Unity of the Virtues'). On the other hand, several writers (including Penner, PR 1973; Irwin, *Plato's Moral Theory*, ch. 4, and *Plato's Ethics*, ch. 6; Taylor, *Protagoras* comm.; Ferejohn, *JHP* 1982) have sought to interpret these sentences literally. While there are differences in detail, these writers agree in interpreting Socrates as maintaining that the different names all pick out the same state of character via non-synonymous designations. Thus courage is that in virtue of which one does the right thing in situations of danger, holiness that in virtue of which one does the right thing in matters of religion etc., and *that in virtue of which* these attributes apply is literally the same state of the individual, specifically the state of knowing what is best for oneself. It should be observed that these writers agree with Vlastos on the substantive account of Socrates' moral psychology; the difference between their views and his is purely a matter of how that psychology is to be described. For Vlastos the names of the specific excellences are names of behavioural tendencies which, while distinct, are necessarily connected to knowledge of the good and therefore to one another; for Penner and the others they are names of that knowledge itself, specifying it via the distinct behavioural tendencies in which it is expressed.

It is the substantive question of moral psychology which is at the heart of the dispute between Socrates and Protagoras. If all the excellences depend on knowledge of the good as Socrates maintains, then the acquisition of that knowledge is crucial in acquiring them, and only someone who can impart that knowledge is competent to teach excellence. If, as Protagoras holds, the excellences are separate attributes, it remains a matter for debate whether there is any systematic method of imparting them. In particular, if courage is, as he maintains, something altogether different from the other virtues, it is plausible that inculcating it will require a kind of training quite distinct from that appropriate to the development of the others, which, being very similar to one another, might be thought likely to be developed by a broadly unitary programme. Protagoras appears to assume that traditional methods of moral instruction, supplemented in some unspecified ways by sophistic teaching, will be adequate (327a–328c). Socrates seeks to show the inadequacy of that conception of moral education.[6]

---

[6] I assume that Socrates is represented as maintaining the thesis of the unity of the virtues, as opposed to a reading of the dialogue on which he is

In the final section of the dialogue (351b ff.), the discussion proceeds by way of examination of a thesis about the relation of pleasure to goodness. Socrates argues that once that thesis is established it can be shown that courage is identical with knowledge of the good and harm resulting from action, good and harm being measured in terms of pleasure and its opposite, distress. The thesis is stated in terms which are indeterminate between the following alternatives: (*a*) pleasure (understood in a wide sense as the predominance of pleasure over distress over a whole life) is the supreme good, (*b*) pleasure (so understood) is the only good, (*c*) the pleasure of any action or situation (understood as the positive contribution of that action or situation to a life in which pleasure predominates over distress) is identical with the goodness of that action or situation.

It is disputed whether Socrates is represented as arguing for that thesis in his own person, and thereby as inferring from it the identity of courage with knowledge, or as arguing merely that either ordinary people, or Protagoras, or both, accept that thesis, and hence that they are committed to the identification of courage with knowledge which it allegedly entails. A decision on that question is inextricable from certain other issues. These include the following.

(*a*) Is Socrates represented as seeking in the dialogue to establish some positive doctrine or doctrines of his own, or merely as critical of the claims of Protagoras to teach excellence? If his purpose is wholly critical, then it would be quite apposite for Plato to represent Protagoras as having no view on the nature of goodness independent of the views of ordinary people, and thereby as committed to whatever Socrates could show to follow from the latter. If, on the other hand, Socrates is represented as arguing for the identification of courage with knowledge as his own view, he must also be represented as maintaining in his own person the premiss from which that conclusion is deduced. It is certain that criticism of the educational claims of the sophists (represented here by

concerned merely to show that Protagoras is committed to accepting that thesis. For justification of that position see the introduction to my commentary, xiv–xvi.

Protagoras) is *one* of Plato's aims in writing the dialogue (see above), but it is far from certain that it is his only aim; on the contrary, the conclusion of the dialogue (especially 361b) suggests that he intends to represent Socrates as seeking to establish views of his own.

(*b*) How is the presentation of Socrates in this dialogue related to that in other dialogues which may be reasonably supposed to have been composed at the same period of Plato's life? There are two dimensions to this question, the first relating directly to the theme of the previous paragraph. If in other dialogues Socrates is exclusively critical, the interpretation of the argument of the *Protagoras* as purely *ad hominem* gains some support, whereas the positive interpretation is strengthened by such evidence as other dialogues provide of Socrates' arguing for his own views. The other relates to the question of hedonism. To the extent to which other dialogues attribute to Socrates attitudes to pleasure which are inconsistent with adherence to the hedonistic thesis of the *Protagoras*, to that extent it becomes more plausible to suppose that in the latter Socrates is represented as arguing *ad hominem*, rather than maintaining the thesis in his own person. These questions are also complicated by considerations of the relative order in which various dialogues were written. Thus if the *Protagoras* was written before the *Gorgias* and *Phaedo*, it is possible to see the hedonism of the former as a Socratic position from which Plato gradually distances himself in the latter two dialogues, whereas if either were written before the *Protagoras* it would be much more difficult to sustain the hypothesis of Socratic commitment to hedonism in that dialogue.

None of these questions has a knock-down answer, as the persistence of lively scholarly debate on them attests. While Socrates' argumentative stance is predominantly critical in the early to middle dialogues, it is not exclusively so. For instance, the *Crito*, a dialogue generally thought to be among the earliest, shows Socrates arguing positively for the thesis that it would be wrong for him to evade his death sentence by escaping from prison, while in the *Meno* (probably slightly later than the *Protagoras*) he argues positively for the identification of excellence with knowledge, the same thesis as, in my view, he maintains in this dialogue. The question of attitudes to hedonism in other dialogues is more complicated. The *Protagoras* is indeed the only dialogue in which Socrates is represented as arguing in favour of any version of hedonism, while in the *Gorgias* and *Phaedo* he argues against certain versions of it. But in neither dialogue is the version of hedonism opposed precisely that defended in the *Protagoras*, and in any case it is likely that both dialogues are somewhat later, allowing the hypothesis of development from a fairly simple hedonistic starting-point to a more nuanced stance on pleasure.[7] Some scholars have suggested that the absolute commitment to justice which Socrates maintains in the *Apology* and *Crito*, both generally agreed to be earlier than the *Protagoras*, must have made the portrayal of a hedonistic Socrates incredible to readers familiar with the earlier works; justice has intrinsic and absolute value for the Socrates of those works, whereas hedonism makes the value of anything other than pleasure derivative and conditional. This objection raises some very complex issues, which cannot be dealt with fully here. It must suffice to say that it is not obvious that the contrast between hedonism and the absolute value of justice is as stark as the objection requires. Justice is certainly an intrinsic good for Socrates, but intrinsic goods are good in virtue of their goodness, which is not incompatible with the claim that their goodness is identical with their pleasantness. If it is objected that it is altogether implausible to claim that justice is intrinsically pleasant, that needs further argument. If by pleasant we understand 'necessarily contributing to an overall pleasant life', then it is at least not obvious that that is not true of justice. Justice is described at *Crito* 47d–48a as an intrinsic good of the soul, as health is of the body; it is not implausible to claim that both are intrinsic goods in virtue of being (*a*) pleasant in themselves, (*b*) such that

---

[7] The position outlined here is defended in detail in Gosling and Taylor, chs. 3–5. For opposed views see e.g. Kahn, *OSAP* 1988 and Weiss, *JHP* 1989 and *AP* 1990. I argue against Kahn's early dating of the *Gorgias* in my commentary, introd. xviii–xx.

their absence is both painful in itself and destructive of other pleasures.

This introduction has attempted to explore some of the intricacies of this complex work, which is peculiarly fascinating not only (though not least) from the abstractly philosophical point of view, but also as an important document of intellectual history and a central piece of evidence for our assessment of the nature of Plato's philosophical activity. It has not attempted to capture the dramatic impact and vividness of characterization which make it one of the most attractive works of Greek literature. Those delights I am happy to leave to the reader.

NOTE ON THE TRANSLATION

THE translation used in this volume is taken from the second (revised) edition of my volume on the *Protagoras* in the Clarendon Plato Series (referred to as 'Taylor, *Protagoras* comm.'). It appears here with minor revisions. Some of the Explanatory Notes are also excerpted (some in abbreviated form, or with emendations) from that volume.

The numbers and letters printed in the margin of the translation, which refer originally to the pages and sections of the sixteenth-century edition of Plato by Henri Estienne (Stephanus), are the standard method of reference to Plato's text. The line numbers in the translation are those of the Oxford Classical Text.

SELECT BIBLIOGRAPHY

Complete Greek Text of Plato

Burnet, J., *Platonis Opera* (5 vols.; Oxford: Clarendon Press (Oxford Classical Texts), 1900–7). *Protagoras* in vol. iii. A new text is in preparation; vol. i, ed. E. A. Duke *et al.*, appeared in 1995.

Complete Translation

Cooper, J. M., ed., *Plato, Complete Works* (Indianapolis: Hackett, 1997).
Jowett, B., *The Dialogues of Plato* (4th edn. (revised D. J. Allan and H. E. Dale); Oxford: Clarendon Press, 1953). *Protagoras* in vol. i.

Editions of Protagoras *with Greek Text*

Adam, J., and Adam, A. M., *Platonis Protagoras* (2nd edn.; Cambridge: Cambridge University Press, 1905). Text with introduction and commentary.
Croiset, A., *Platon, Protagoras*, (vol. iii, part 1 of complete Budé edn. of Plato; Paris: Les Belles Lettres, 1923). Text with French translation, introduction, and some notes.
Denyer, N., *Plato, Protagoras* (Cambridge: Cambridge University Press, 2008). Text with introduction and commentary.
Lamb, W. R. M., *Plato, Laches, Protagoras, Meno, Euthydemus* (vol. ii of complete Loeb edn. of Plato; London and Cambridge, Mass.: Harvard University Press, 1924). Text with English translation, introduction, and notes.

Translations of Protagoras

Guthrie, W. K. C., *Plato, Protagoras and Meno* (Harmondsworth: Penguin Books, 1956). Translation and introduction. Translation reprinted in Hamilton and Cairns, op. cit.
Hubbard, B. A. F., and Karnofsky, E. S., *Plato's Protagoras: A Socratic Commentary* (London: Duckworth, 1982). Translation with commentary in the form of questions.
Lombardo, S., and Bell, K., *Plato, Protagoras* (Indianapolis and Cambridge: Hackett, 1992). Translation with notes. Introduction by M. Frede.

BIBLIOGRAPHY

Taylor, C. C. W., *Plato, Protagoras* (2nd (rev.) edn.; Oxford: Clarendon Press, 1991). Translation with introduction and commentary.

Vlastos, G. (ed.), *Plato, Protagoras: Jowett's Translation Revised by Martin Ostwald* (Indianapolis and New York: Bobbs-Merrill, 1956). Translation with notes; introduction by the editor.

General Works on Plato

Field, G. C., *Plato and His Contemporaries* (London: Methuen, 1930).

Fine, G., ed., *The Oxford Handbook of Plato* (Oxford: Oxford University Press, 2008).

Gosling, J. C. B., *Plato* (London and Boston: Routledge and Kegan Paul, 1973).

Irwin, T., *Plato's Ethics* (New York and Oxford: Oxford University Press, 1995). Ch. 6 deals with the *Protagoras*.

Kraut, R. (ed.), *The Cambridge Companion to Plato* (Cambridge: Cambridge University Press, 1992).

Rowe, C. J., *Plato* (Brighton: Harvester Press, 1984).

Works on Socrates

Ahbel-Rappe, S., and Kamtekar, R., eds., *A Companion to Socrates* (Malden, MA: Blackwell, 2006).

Benson, H. H. (ed.), *Essays on the Philosophy of Socrates* (New York and Oxford: Oxford University Press, 1992).

Brickhouse, T. D., and Smith, N. D., *Plato's Socrates* (New York and Oxford: Oxford University Press, 1994).

Gower, B. S., and Stokes, M. C. (eds.), *Socratic Questions* (London and New York: Routledge, 1992).

Guthrie, W. K. C., *A History of Greek Philosophy*, iii, part 2 (Cambridge: Cambridge University Press, 1969). Published separately 1971 under title *Socrates*.

Taylor, C. C. W., *Socrates* (Oxford: Oxford University Press, 1998).

Vlastos, G. (ed.), *The Philosophy of Socrates: A Collection of Critical Essays* (Garden City, NY: Doubleday, 1971).

—— *Socrates, Ironist and Moral Philosopher* (Cambridge: Cambridge University Press, 1991).

—— *Socratic Studies* (ed. M. Burnyeat) (Cambridge: Cambridge University Press, 1994).

BIBLIOGRAPHY

Works on the Sophists

Guthrie, *A History of Greek Philosophy*, iii, part 1. Published separately 1971 under title *The Sophists*.

Kerferd, G. B., *The Sophistic Movement* (Cambridge: Cambridge University Press, 1981).

—— (ed.), *The Sophists and Their Legacy* (*Hermes* Einzelschriften 44; Wiesbaden: Franz Steiner Verlag, 1981).

Works on the *Protagoras*

Frede, D., 'The Impossibility of Perfection: Socrates' Criticism of Simonides' Poem in the Protagoras', *RM* 39 (1985–6), 729–53.

Irwin, T., *Plato's Moral Theory* (Oxford: Clarendon Press, 1977), ch. 4.

Havlíček, A., and Karfík, F., eds., *Plato's Protagoras, Proceedings of the Third Symposium Platonicum Pragense* (Prague: Oikoumenē, 2003).

Kahn, C. H., 'On the Relative Date of the *Gorgias* and the *Protagoras*', *OSAP* 6 (1988), 69–102.

—— 'Plato and Socrates in the *Protagoras*', *Methexis*, Revista Argentina de Filosofía Antigua, 1 (1988), 33–51.

Nussbaum, M. C., *The Fragility of Goodness* (Cambridge: Cambridge University Press, 1986), ch. 4.

Penner, T., 'The Unity of Virtue', *PR* 82 (1973), 35–68

Rutherford, R., 'Unifying the *Protagoras*', in A. Barker and M. Warner (eds.), *The Language of the Cave* (*Apeiron*, 25.4 (1992)), 133–56, repr. with emendations in Rutherford, *The Art of Plato* (London: Duckworth, 1995), ch. 5.

Santas, G., 'Plato's *Protagoras* and Explanations of Weakness', *PR* 75 (1966), 3–33, repr. in Vlastos (ed.), *The Philosophy of Socrates*, in G. Mortimore (ed.), *Weakness of Will* (London: Macmillan, 1971), and with minor revisions in Santas, *Socrates* (London, Boston, and Henley: Routledge and Kegan Paul, 1979), ch. 7.

Saunders, T. J., 'Protagoras and Plato on Punishment', in Kerferd (ed.), *The Sophists and Their Legacy*, 129–41.

Schofield, M., 'Socrates versus Protagoras', in Gower and Stokes (eds.), *Socratic Questions*, 122–36.

Vlastos, G., 'Socrates on Acrasia', *Phoenix*, 23 (1969), 71–88, repr. in Vlastos, *Studies in Greek Philosophy*, ii, *Socrates, Plato, and Their Tradition* (ed. D. W. Graham) (Princeton: Princeton University Press, 1995).

—— 'The Unity of the Virtues in the *Protagoras*', *RM* 25 (1971–2),

415–58, repr. with emendations and additions in Vlastos, *Platonic Studies* (2nd edn.; Princeton: Princeton University Press, 1981).

Weiss, R., 'The Hedonic Calculus in the *Protagoras* and *Phaedo*', *JHP* 27 (1989), 511–29.

—— 'Hedonism in the *Protagoras* and the Sophist's Guarantee', *AP* 10 (1990), 17–39.

Other Works

Dover, K. J., *Aristophanes, Clouds* (Oxford: Clarendon Press, 1968). Introduction section 5 repr. in Vlastos (ed.), *The Philosophy of Socrates*.

—— *Greek Homosexuality* (London: Duckworth, 1978; 2nd edn. 1989).

Ferejohn, M. T., 'The Unity of Virtue and the Objects of Socratic Enquiry', *JHP* 20 (1982), 1–21.

Gosling, J. C. B., and Taylor, C. C. W., *The Greeks on Pleasure* (Oxford: Clarendon Press, 1982).

Kahn, C. H., 'The Origins of Social Contract Theory in the Fifth Century B.C.', in Kerferd (ed.), *The Sophists and Their Legacy*, 92–108.

Further Reading in Oxford World's Classics

Plato, *Defence of Socrates, Euthyphro, Crito*, tr. David Gallop.

—— *Gorgias*, tr. Robin Waterfield.

—— *Meno and Other Dialogues*, tr. Robin Waterfield.

—— *Phaedo*, tr. David Gallop.

—— *Phaedrus*, tr. Robin Waterfield.

—— *Republic*, tr. Robin Waterfield.

—— *Selected Myths*, ed. Catalin Partenie.

—— *Symposium*, tr. Robin Waterfield.

—— *Timaeus and Critias*, tr. Robin Waterfield, ed. Andrew Gregory.

The First Philosophers. The Presocratics and the Sophists, tr. Robin Waterfield.

PROTAGORAS

FRIEND. Hello, Socrates; what have you been doing? No 309a
need to ask; you've been chasing around after that handsome young fellow Alcibiades.* Certainly when I saw him
just recently he struck me as still a fine-looking man,
but a man all the same, Socrates (just between ourselves), with his beard already coming.   5

SOCRATES. Well, what of it? Aren't you an admirer of
Homer? He says that the most delightful age is that at   b
which a young man gets his first beard, just the age
Alcibiades is now, in fact.

FRIEND. Well, how are things at the moment? Have you
been with him? How is the young fellow disposed towards you?

SOCRATES. Very well, it seems to me, not least today. For   5
he took my part and said a lot of things on my behalf,
and in fact I've only just left him. But I've something
remarkable to tell you; though he was there, I didn't
take much notice of him, and on a number of occasions
I forgot about him altogether.

FRIEND. How on earth could such a thing have happened   c
to the two of you? You surely haven't met someone even
finer-looking, in this city at least.

SOCRATES. Yes, far finer-looking.

FRIEND. What? A citizen or a foreigner?   5

SOCRATES. A foreigner.

FRIEND. Where from?

SOCRATES. Abdera.

FRIEND. And this foreigner struck you as such a fine-
looking man that he was even finer than the son of
Cleinias?   10

SOCRATES. Well surely, my dear fellow, what is wisest is
always finer?

3

FRIEND. Oh, you mean that you've just met some wise man, Socrates?

d SOCRATES. The wisest man alive, I believe, if you agree that that description fits Protagoras.

FRIEND. What's that you say? Is Protagoras in the city?

SOCRATES. He's been here for two days now.

5 FRIEND. And you've just come from talking to him?

310a SOCRATES. Yes indeed. I said a lot to him and he to me.

FRIEND. Well, if there's nothing else you have to do, why don't you tell us about your conversation? Sit down here, and let the slave there get up and make room for you.

5 SOCRATES. Certainly. I shall be glad if you'll listen.

FRIEND. And we shall be grateful to you, if you'll tell us.

SOCRATES. That's a favour on either side. Well, listen then.

310a8–314c2 Socrates narrates how a young friend, Hippocrates, called on him early in the morning to ask for an introduction to Protagoras. He questions Hippocrates on what he hopes to learn from Protagoras and finds that he has no clear idea of what the sophist has to teach. The only suggestion Hippocrates makes, that Protagoras teaches one how to be an effective speaker, does not, Socrates argues, differentiate sophists from other experts, e.g. musicians. Socrates warns Hippocrates of the dangers of submitting to education without an adequate conception of its content.

Last night, just before daybreak, Hippocrates,* the son of Apollodorus and brother of Phason, began knocking very

b loudly on the door with his stick, and when someone opened it he came straight in in a great hurry, calling out

5 loudly, 'Socrates, are you awake or asleep?' I recognized his voice and said, 'It's Hippocrates; no bad news, I hope?' 'Nothing but good news,' he said. 'Splendid,' I said; 'what is it, then? What brings you here so early?' He came and stood beside me; 'Protagoras has come,' he said. 'He came the day before yesterday,' I said; 'have you only just heard?' 'Yes, indeed,' he said; 'yesterday evening.'

c As he said this he felt for the bed and sat down at my

4

feet. 'Yes, it was yesterday evening, when I got back very late from Oinoe. My slave Satyrus ran away; I was going to tell you that I was going after him, but something else put it out of my head. When I got back, and we had had supper and were just going to bed, it was then that my brother told me that Protagoras had come. Late as it was, I immediately got up to come and tell you, but then I realized that it was far too late at night; but as soon as I had had a sleep and got rid of my tiredness, I got up straight away and came over here, as you see.'

I knew him to be a spirited and excitable character, so I said, 'What's all this to you? Protagoras hasn't done you any wrong, has he?'

He laughed. 'By heavens, he has, Socrates. He is the only man who is wise, but he doesn't make me wise too.'

'Oh yes, he will,' I said; 'If you give him money and use a little persuasion, he'll make you wise as well.'

'I wish to God', he said, 'that that was all there was to it. I'd use every penny of my own, and of my friends too. But it's just that that I've come to you about now, so that you can put in a word for me with him. First of all, I'm too young, and then I've never seen Protagoras nor heard him speak; for I was still a child when he came here before. But you know, Socrates, everybody speaks highly of the man, and says that he's a wonderfully clever speaker. Why don't we go to him, so as to catch him at home? He's staying, so I've heard, with Callias the son of Hipponicus. Do let's go.'

'Don't let's go there yet,' I said; 'it's still early. Let's go out into the courtyard here, and take a turn to pass the time till it gets light, and then let's go. Protagoras spends most of the time indoors, so you needn't worry, we'll probably find him in.'

Then we got up, went out into the courtyard and strolled about. In order to test Hippocrates I began to examine him and ask him questions. 'Tell me, Hippocrates,' I said. 'You are now planning to go to Protagoras and give him money in payment for services to yourself. What sort of man is it that you're going to, and what sort of man are you going to become as a result? Suppose you had been

thinking of going to your namesake Hippocrates of Cos,*
of the medical guild, and giving him money in payment
for services to yourself. If someone had then asked, "Tell
c me, for what service are you paying Hippocrates?" what
would you have answered?'

'I should have said for his services as a doctor.'

'And what would you hope to become as a result?'

'A doctor.'

'And suppose you had been thinking of going to Polycleitus of Argos or Pheidias of Athens and giving them
5 money in payment for services to yourself. If someone had
then asked you, "What is the service for which you are
going to pay this money to Polycleitus and Pheidias?"*
what would you have answered?'

'I should have said for their services as sculptors.'

'And what would you hope to become yourself?'

'A sculptor, obviously.'

d 'Well now,' I said, 'you and I are prepared at this moment
to go to Protagoras and pay him money for services to
you, if our own resources are sufficient to persuade him,
5 and, if not, to spend our friends' money as well. If somebody saw how desperately eager we are in this matter and
asked us what service we were going to pay Protagoras
e for, what should we reply? What other name do we hear
applied to Protagoras? I mean, the way Pheidias is called
a sculptor and Homer is called a poet, is there any name
of that sort which we hear applied to Protagoras?'

'Well, a sophist* is what they call him, anyhow, Socrates,' he said.

5 'So it's for his services as a sophist that we're going to
pay him?'

'Certainly.'

312a 'Well now, suppose someone asked you, "And what do
you yourself hope to become as a result of your association with Protagoras?"'

He blushed—day was already beginning to break, so
that I could see him—and replied, 'If it's like what we said
before, then obviously I should be hoping to become a
sophist.'

'But, for heaven's sake,' I said, 'wouldn't you be ashamed   5
to present yourself to the world as a sophist?'

'Of course I should, Socrates, if I'm to be quite frank.'*

'But then perhaps that isn't the sort of study you expect
to have with Protagoras, but rather the sort you had with   b
the reading-master* and the music teacher and the trainer.
You didn't learn any of those things in a technical way,
with a view to becoming a professional yourself, but simply for their educational value, as an amateur and a gen-
tleman should.'

'Exactly,' he said. 'I think that study with Protagoras is   5
rather of that sort.'

'Do you realize, then, what you are going to do,' I said,
'or don't you?'

'What do you mean?'

'I mean that you are going to entrust your soul* to the   c
care of a man who is, as you agree, a sophist. But I should
be surprised if you even know what a sophist is. And yet
if you don't know that, you don't even know what it is
that you're handing your soul over to, nor even whether
it's something good or something bad.'

'Well, at least I think I know,' he said.

'Tell me, then, what do you think a sophist is?'   5

'Well, I think', he said, 'a sophist is, as the name implies,* one who is knowledgeable in learned matters.'

'Surely', I said, 'you can say the same about painters
and carpenters, that they are knowledgeable in learned   d
matters. But if someone asked us which learned matters
painters are knowledgeable about, we should say that they
are knowledgeable about the making of pictures, and so
in the other cases. Now if we were asked which learned
matters the sophist is knowledgeable about, what should
we say? What craft is he master of?'   5

'What answer should we give, Socrates, except to say
that he is master of the craft of making people clever
speakers?'

'Perhaps that would be true,' I said, 'but it's not enough;
our answer invites the further question: "What is it that
the sophist makes you a clever speaker about?" I mean,   e

7

the music teacher no doubt makes you a clever speaker about what he teaches you, namely music. Isn't that so?'*

'Yes.'

'Well then, what is it that the sophist makes you a clever speaker about?'

'Obviously, about what he knows.'

5   'Presumably. What then is this knowledge which the sophist himself possesses and which he imparts to his pupil?'

'Really,' he said, 'I find I've no more to say.'

313a   Then I said, 'Well, do you realize the danger that you are going to expose yourself to in taking a chance like this? If you had to entrust your physical health to some-

5   one, for good or ill, you would weigh up the matter very carefully, and call on your friends and relations for advice and take a long time to decide. But now in a matter which concerns something which you value more highly than your body, I mean your soul, on whose condition your whole fate depends for good or ill, you haven't sought the

b   advice of your father or your brother or of any of us who are your friends as to whether or not to entrust your soul to this stranger who has just arrived. No, you heard of his arrival yesterday evening, so you tell me, and come along at daybreak without any thought or advice on whether

5   you ought to entrust yourself to him or not, prepared to spend your own money and your friends' as well, since you've already decided, apparently, that you must at all costs become a pupil of Protagoras, whom you neither

c   know, as you admit, nor have you ever spoken to him. You call him a sophist, and it turns out that you don't even know what a sophist is; and yet that's the man to whom you're going to entrust yourself.'

When I had finished he said, 'It seems so, Socrates, from what you say.'

5   'Well now, Hippocrates, the sophist happens to be a sort of merchant or pedlar of goods for the nourishment of the soul; at least he seems to me something of that sort.'

'What sort of thing nourishes the soul, Socrates?'

8

'Learning, surely,' I said. 'And we have to make sure that the sophist doesn't take us in by his praise of his goods, as merchants and pedlars of ordinary food do. For they don't know whether the stuff they are hawking around is good or bad for you, but they say that everything in their stock is good. Their customers don't know either, unless one of them happens to be a trainer or a doctor. In the same way these people who make their living by hawking learning from city to city and selling to whoever wants to buy say that everything in their stock is good, but perhaps even some of them, my dear fellow, might not know whether what they are selling is good or bad for the soul. It's the same for their customers, unless one of them happens to be a doctor of the soul. So if you happen to know which of their wares is good and which is bad, it's safe for you to buy learning from Protagoras or anyone else; but if not, then watch out, my friend. Don't take chances in a matter of such importance. For you know, there's much more risk in buying learning than in buying food. If you buy food or drink from a pedlar or a merchant you can carry it away in another container, and before you actually eat or drink it you can set it down at home and call in an expert and take his advice on what you ought to eat or drink and what you ought not, and how much, and when you ought to take it. So there is no great risk in buying. But you can't carry learning away in a jar; you have to put down the price and take the learning into your soul right away. By the time you go away you have already assimilated it, and got the harm or the benefit. So let's consider this along with our elders; for we are still too young to settle such an important matter. But now, let's go and listen to Protagoras as we set out to do, and afterwards let's consult some others. For Protagoras isn't there alone; Hippias of Elis is there too, and I think Prodicus of Ceos as well, and many other wise men.'

314c3–317e2   *Arrival of Socrates and Hippocrates at the house of Callias; description of the scene. Introductory conversation with Protagoras.*

We agreed on that, and went off. When we got to the
5   doorway, we stood there talking about some subject which
had come up on the way. As we didn't want to break off
the discussion, but preferred to reach a conclusion and
then go in, we stood in the doorway talking until we
reached agreement. I think that the porter, a eunuch, must
d   have overheard us, and perhaps he was annoyed at the
throngs of people that the number of sophists was bringing to the house. At any rate, when we knocked at the
door, he opened it and saw us. 'Ah, sophists,' he said;
'he's busy,' and at the same time he slammed the door
5   with both hands as hard as he could. We began knocking
again, and he kept the door closed and said, 'Didn't you
hear? He's busy.' 'My dear sir,' I said, 'we haven't come
e   to see Callias, nor are we sophists. Don't worry. We've
come to see Protagoras. Just tell them we've come.' So
eventually, with great reluctance, the fellow opened the
door to us.

    When we came in we found Protagoras walking in the
5   colonnade, and ranged on one side of him were Callias
315a the son of Hipponicus* and his half-brother Paralus the
son of Pericles and Charmides* the son of Glaucon, and on
the other Pericles' other son Xanthippus and Philippides*
the son of Philomelus and Antimoerus of Mende, who has
5   the highest reputation of any of Protagoras' pupils and is
studying with him professionally, with a view to becoming a sophist. Those who were following them listening
to the conversation seemed mostly to be foreigners—
Protagoras collects them from every city he passes through,
charming them with his voice like Orpheus, and they follow the sound of his voice quite spellbound—but there
b   were some Athenians in the procession* too. I was abso-
lutely delighted by this procession, to see how careful they
5   were that nobody ever got in Protagoras' way, but whenever he and his companions turned round, those followers
of his turned smartly outwards in formation to left and
right, wheeled round and so every time formed up in perfect
order behind him.

c   'And after him I recognized',* as Homer says, Hippias of

Elis, sitting in a chair in the opposite colonnade. Around him were sitting on benches Eryximachus* the son of Acumenus and Phaedrus* from Myrrinus and Andron the son of Androtion and a number of foreigners, fellow citizens of Hippias and others. They seemed to be asking Hippias questions on science and astronomy, and he was sitting in his chair giving a detailed decision on every question.

'And then I saw Tantalus too', for Prodicus of Ceos was also in town. He was in a room which Hipponicus previously used as a store-room, but now because of the number of visitors Callias had cleared it out too and turned it into a guest-room. Prodicus was still in bed, wrapped up in a great many sheepskins and blankets, as far as I could see. On the beds next to his sat Pausanias* from Cerameis, and with him a young lad, a fine boy in my opinion, and certainly very fine-looking. I think I heard that his name was Agathon,* and I shouldn't be surprised if Pausanias were in love with him. There was that lad, and the two Adeimantuses, the son of Cepis* and the son of Leucolophides, and there seemed to be some others; but I couldn't catch from outside what they were talking about, though I was very eager to hear Prodicus—for I think that he is a wonderful man, and very learned—but his deep voice made such a booming noise in the room that the words themselves were indistinct.

We had just come in, when there came in behind us the handsome Alcibiades, as you call him, and I agree, and Critias the son of Callaeschrus.

When we came in we spent a few moments looking at all this, and then we went over to Protagoras, and I said, 'Protagoras, Hippocrates here and I have come to see you.'

'Do you want to talk to me alone', he said, 'or in the presence of the others?'

'As far as we're concerned,' I said, 'it makes no difference. You decide once you've heard what we've come about.'

'What is it, then, that you've come about?' he asked.

'Hippocrates here is an Athenian, the son of Apollodorus, of a great and wealthy family, and in natural ability he

c   seems the equal of anyone of his age. I think that he wants
to become eminent in public life, and he thinks that that
would be most likely to happen if he were to become a
pupil of yours. So perhaps you would now consider
whether you think you ought to talk to us about this in
private, or in the presence of others.'

5   'You show a very proper consideration for me, Socrates,' he said. 'A foreigner who comes to great cities and
persuades the best of the young men to abandon the so-
d   ciety of others, kinsmen or acquaintances, old or young,
and associate with himself for their own improvement—
someone who does that has to be careful. He becomes as
a result the object of a great deal of resentment and hostility, and of many attacks. I maintain that the craft of the
5   sophist is an ancient one, but that its practitioners in ancient
times, for fear of giving offence, adopted the subterfuge of
disguising it as some other craft, as Homer and Hesiod
and Simonides did with poetry, and Orpheus and Musaeus
and their followers with religious rites and prophecies.
Some, I have heard, went in for physical training, like Iccus*
10 e   of Taras and, in our own day, Herodicus* of Selymbria
(originally of Megara), as good a sophist as any. Your
fellow citizen Agathocles, a great sophist, used music and
literature as a cover, and so did Pythocleides* of Ceos and
5   many others. All of them, as I say, used these crafts as a
317a screen out of fear of resentment. But I disagree with them
all over this; for I don't think that they succeeded in their
aim; they didn't deceive the people in power in the various
cities, which was the point of those subterfuges, since the
5   mass of the people don't really notice anything, but just
repeat whatever their rulers tell them. If you can't escape
by running away, but merely bring yourself out into the
open, then it's foolish even to try, and bound to make
b   people much more hostile to you, for they think that
someone who behaves like that is a scoundrel on top of
everything else. So I have gone quite the opposite way
from these others, and I admit that I am a sophist and
5   that I educate people; I think that an admission of that
kind is a better precaution than a denial. And I've taken

other precautions as well, so that, touch wood, I've never
come to any harm through admitting to being a sophist.   c
And yet I've been practising the craft for many years*
(and indeed I'm a good age now, I'm old enough to be the
father of any of you).* So I much prefer, if you please, to
talk about these things in the presence of all who are
here.'   5

I suspected that he wanted to put on a performance in
front of Prodicus and Hippias and show off because we   d
had turned up to admire him, so I said, 'Why don't we ask
Prodicus and Hippias and the people with them to come
over too, and listen?'

'By all means,' said Protagoras.

'Would you like us to put out some seats', said Callias,   5
'so that you can talk sitting down?'

It was agreed that we should do that. We were all pleased
at the prospect of hearing wise men talk, and we took the
benches and beds ourselves and arranged them beside   10
Hippias, as the benches were set out there already; mean-   e
while Callias and Alcibiades fetched Prodicus from his
bed and came along with him and those who were with
him.

317e3–320c1 *Socrates asks Protagoras what Hippocrates
will learn from him. Protagoras replies that he will teach
him how to attain success in public and private life.
Socrates interprets this as a claim to be able to teach men
how to be good citizens, an account of his activity which
is accepted by Protagoras. Socrates then gives two reasons
for thinking it impossible to teach that: (a) on matters of
policy, as opposed to technical questions, the Athenians
do not regard anyone as an expert; (b) men who are ac-
knowledged to be outstandingly good citizens have failed
to make their sons equally good.*

When we were all sitting down Protagoras said, 'Now
that these others are here, Socrates, you might say some-   5
thing about what you mentioned to me a short time ago
on your young friend's behalf.'

318a 'I'll begin', I said, 'just where I did last time, by saying what we've come about. Hippocrates here is anxious to become your pupil; so he says that he would be glad to know what benefit he will derive from associating with

5 you. That's the sum of our conversation so far.'

'Young man,' replied Protagoras, 'if you associate with me, this is the benefit you will gain: the very day you become my pupil you will go home a better man, and the same the next day; and every day you will continue to make progress.'

b 'There's nothing remarkable in that,' I said. 'It's just what you'd expect, since even you, old and wise as you are, would become a better man if someone taught you

5 something that you happened not to know. Don't just answer like that, but suppose that Hippocrates suddenly changed his mind and was anxious to study with that young man who has recently come to the city, Zeuxippus*

c of Heraclea, and came to him as he has now done to you, and heard him say what you have just said, that every day he will improve himself and become a better man through studying with him. If he asked, "In what respect do you

5 say that I'll be better? What will I improve at?" Zeuxippus would say, "At painting". And if he went to Orthagoras* of Thebes and heard him say what you've said and asked him in what respect he would become better day by day through studying with him, Orthagoras would say "At playing the aulos". In just the same way, will you please

d answer the young man and me, when I put the question on his behalf: "If Hippocrates becomes a pupil of Protagoras, and goes away a better man on the very day he becomes a pupil, and makes similar progress every day, what will he be better at, and in what respect will he make progress?"'

5 Protagoras answered, 'You have put a good question, Socrates, and I like answering people who do that. If Hippocrates comes to me he won't have the same experience as he would have had had he gone to any other

e sophist. The others maltreat young men; they come to them to get away from school studies, and they take them and pitch them back into those studies against their will, and teach them arithmetic and astronomy and geometry and music and literature'—and as he said this he looked at Hippias—'but if he comes to me he won't learn anything but what he came for. What I teach is the proper management of one's own affairs, how best to run one's household, and the management of public affairs, how to make the most effective contribution to the affairs of the city both by word and action.'

'Have I understood you correctly, then?' I said. 'You seem to me to be talking about the art of running a city, and to be promising to make men into good citizens.'*

'That, Socrates,' he said, 'is precisely what I undertake to do.'

'It's a splendid thing to have discovered,' I said, 'if you have in fact discovered how to do it (for I shall not say, particularly to you, anything other than what I really think). I didn't think that that was something that could be taught, but since you say that you teach it I don't see how I can doubt you. Why I think that it can't be taught or handed on from one man to another, I ought to explain. I say, as do the rest of the Greeks, that the Athenians are wise. Well, I observe that when a decision has to be taken at the state assembly about some matter of building, they send for the builders to give their advice about the buildings, and when it concerns shipbuilding they send for the shipwrights, and similarly in every case where they are dealing with a subject which they think can be learned and taught. But if anyone else tries to give advice, whom they don't regard as an expert, no matter how handsome or wealthy or well-born he is, they still will have none of him, but jeer at him and create an uproar, until either the would-be speaker is shouted down and gives up of his own accord, or else the police drag him away or put him out on the order of the presidents. That's the way they act in what they regard as a technical matter. But when some matter of state policy comes up for consideration, anyone can get up and give his opinion, be he carpenter, smith or cobbler, merchant or ship-owner, rich or poor, noble or

5   low-born, and no one objects to them as they did to those I mentioned just now, that they are trying to give advice about something which they never learnt, nor ever had any instruction in. So it's clear that they don't regard that

e   as something that can be taught. And not only is this so in public affairs, but in private life our wisest and best citizens are unable to hand on to others the excellence* which they possess. For Pericles, the father of these young men, educated them very well in those subjects in which

320a there were teachers, but he neither instructs them himself nor has them instructed by anyone else in those matters in which he is himself wise; no, they wander about on their own like sacred cattle looking for pasture, hoping to pick up excellence by chance. Or take the case of Cleinias,* the

5   younger brother of Alcibiades here. Pericles, whom I mentioned just now, is his guardian, and no doubt for fear he should be corrupted by Alcibiades he took him away from him and sent him to be brought up in Ariphron's* house;

b   and before six months were up he gave him back to Alcibiades, not knowing what to do with him. And I could mention many others, good men themselves, who never made anyone better, either their own families, or anyone

5   else. So when I consider these facts, Protagoras, I don't think that excellence can be taught. But then when I hear you say that you teach it, I am swayed once again and think that there must be something in what you say, as I regard you as someone of great experience and learning, who has made discoveries himself. So if you can show us more clearly that excellence can be taught, please don't

c   grudge us your proof, but proceed.'

    'Certainly I shall not grudge it you, Socrates,' he said. 'But would you rather that I showed you by telling a story (as an older man speaking to his juniors) or by going through a systematic exposition?'

5   Several of those who were sitting around asked him to proceed in whichever way he preferred. 'Well,' he said, 'I think that it will be more enjoyable to tell you a story.'

320c8–328d2 *Protagoras' reply to Socrates' objections.*
  A. Reply to Obj. I (Athenians do not recognize experts

*in political matters): (i) Story of Prometheus (320c8–
322d5), (ii) Explanation and expansion of story
(322d5–324d1).*

B. *Reply to Obj. II (Good citizens do not teach their
sons to be good): (324d2–328c2).*

C. *Summary: (328c3–d2).**

'Once upon a time there were just the gods; mortal beings
did not yet exist. And when the appointed time came for   d
them to come into being too, the gods moulded them
within the earth, mixing together earth and fire and their
compounds. And when they were about to bring them out
into the light of day, they appointed Prometheus and   5
Epimetheus to equip each kind with the powers it required. Epimetheus asked Prometheus to let him assign
the powers himself. "Once I have assigned them", he said,
"you can inspect them"; so Prometheus agreed, and Epimetheus assigned the powers. To some creatures he gave   e
strength, but not speed, while he equipped the weaker
with speed. He gave some claws or horns, and for those
without them he devised some other power for their preservation. To those whom he made of small size, he gave
winged flight, or a dwelling underground; to those that he 321a
made large, he gave their size itself as a protection. And
in the same way he distributed all the other things, bal-
ancing one against another. This he did to make sure that
no species should be wiped out; and when he had made
them defences against mutual destruction, he devised for
them protection against the elements, clothing them with
thick hair and tough skins, so as to withstand cold and   5
heat, and also to serve each kind as their own natural
bedding when they lay down to sleep. And he shod some   b
with hooves, and others with tough, bloodless skin. Then
he assigned different kinds of food to the different species;
some were to live on pasture, others on the fruits of trees,
others on roots, and some he made to prey on other creatures for their food. These he made less prolific, but to
those on whom they preyed he gave a large increase, as a
means of preserving the species.

'Now Epimetheus, not being altogether wise, didn't   c

notice that he had used up all the powers on the non-rational creatures; so last of all he was left with human kind, quite unprovided for, and he was at a loss what to do. As he was racking his brains Prometheus came to inspect the distribution, and saw the other creatures well provided for in every way, while man was naked and unshod, without any covering for his bed or any fangs or claws; and already the appointed day was at hand, on which man too had to come out of the earth to the light of day. Prometheus was at his wits' end to find a means of preservation for mankind, so he stole from Hephaestus and Athena their technical skill along with the use of fire—for it was impossible for anyone to acquire or make use of that skill without fire—and that was what he gave to man. That is how man acquired his practical skill, but he did not yet have skill in running a city; Zeus kept watch over that. Prometheus had no time to penetrate the citadel of Zeus—moreover the guards of Zeus were terrible—but he made his way by stealth into the workshop which Athena and Hephaestus shared for the practice of their arts, and stole Hephaestus' art of working with fire, and the other art which Athena* possesses, and gave them to men. And as a result man was well provided with resources for his life, but afterwards, so it is said, thanks to Epimetheus, Prometheus paid the penalty for theft.

'Since man thus shared in a divine gift, first of all through his kinship with the gods he was the only creature to worship them, and he began to erect altars and images of the gods. Then he soon developed the use of articulate speech and of words, and discovered how to make houses and clothes and shoes and bedding and how to get food from the earth.* Thus equipped, men lived at the beginning in scattered units, and there were no cities; so they began to be destroyed by the wild beasts, since they were altogether weaker. Their practical art was sufficient to provide food, but insufficient for fighting against the beasts —for they did not yet possess the art of running a city, of which the art of warfare is part—and so they sought to come together and save themselves by founding cities. Now when they came together, they treated each other with injustice, not possessing the art of running a city, so they scattered and began to be destroyed once again. So Zeus, fearing that our race would be wholly wiped out, sent Hermes bringing conscience and justice to mankind, to be the principles of organization of cities and the bonds of friendship. Now Hermes asked Zeus about the manner in which he was to give conscience and justice to men: "Shall I distribute these in the same way as the arts? These are distributed thus: one doctor is sufficient for many laymen, and so with the other experts. Shall I give justice and conscience to men in that way too, or distribute them to all?"

'"To all," said Zeus, "and let all share in them; for cities could not come into being, if only a few shared in them as in the other arts. And lay down on my authority a law that he who cannot share in conscience and justice is to be killed as a plague on the city." So that, Socrates, is why when there is a question about how to do well in carpentry or any other expertise, everyone including the Athenians thinks it right that only a few should give advice, and won't put up with advice from anyone else, as you say—and quite right, too, in my view—but when it comes to consideration of how to do well in running the city, which must proceed entirely through justice and soundness of mind, they are right to accept advice from anyone, since it is incumbent on everyone to share in that sort of excellence, or else there can be no city at all.* That is the reason for it, Socrates.

'Just in case you still have any doubts that in fact everyone thinks that every man shares in justice and the rest of the excellence of a citizen, here's an extra bit of evidence. In the case of the other skills, as you say, if anyone says he's a good aulos-player or good at any other art when he isn't, they either laugh at him or get angry at him, and his family come and treat him like a madman. But in the case of justice and the rest of the excellence of a citizen, even if they know someone to be unjust, if he himself admits

5 it before everyone, they regard that sort of truthfulness as madness, though they called it sound sense before, and they say that everybody must say that he is just whether he is or not, and anyone who doesn't pretend to be just must be mad. For they think that everyone must possess it to some extent or other, or else not be among men at

c all.

'On the point, then, that they are right to accept advice from anyone about this sort of excellence in the belief that

5 everyone shares in it, that is all I have to say. I shall next try to show that they think that it does not come by nature or by luck, but that it can be taught, and that everyone who has it has it from deliberate choice.* In the case of undesirable characteristics which people think are

d due to nature or chance, nobody gets annoyed at people who have them or corrects or teaches or punishes them, to make them any different, but they pity them; for instance, is anyone silly enough to try treating the ugly or the small or the weak in any of those ways? No, that sort

5 of thing, I think, they know comes about, fair and foul alike, by nature and by chance. But when it comes to the good qualities that people acquire by deliberate choice, and

e by practice and teaching, if someone doesn't have them, but the opposite bad qualities, it's then that people get

324a annoyed and punish and correct him. One such quality is injustice and impiety and in a word whatever is the opposite of the excellence of a citizen. There everyone gets annoyed with anyone who does wrong, and corrects him, clearly because it's something which you acquire by deliberate choice and learning. For if you care to consider,

5 Socrates, the effect which punishment can possibly have on the wrongdoer, that will itself convince you that people think that excellence is something which can be trained. For no one punishes a wrongdoer with no other thought

b in mind than that he did wrong, unless he is retaliating unthinkingly like an animal. Someone who aims to punish in a rational way doesn't chastise on account of the past misdeed—for that wouldn't undo what is already

5 done—but for the sake of the future, so that neither the

wrongdoer himself, nor anyone else who sees him punished, will do wrong again. This intention shows his belief
that excellence can be produced by education; at least his
aim in punishing is to deter. Now this opinion is shared
by everyone who administers chastisement either in a   c
private or in a public capacity. And everyone chastises
and punishes those whom they think guilty of wrongdoing, not least your fellow citizens, the Athenians; so
according to this argument the Athenians are among those
who think that excellence can be trained and taught. It   5
seems to me, Socrates, that I have now adequately shown
that your fellow citizens are right to accept the advice of
smiths and cobblers on political matters, and also that
they regard excellence as something that can be taught
and trained.*   d

'That still leaves us with your problem about good men,
why it is that they teach their sons and make them knowledgeable in those subjects where there are teachers, but as   5
far as concerns that excellence which they themselves
possess, they don't make their sons any better than anyone else.* On this point, Socrates, I shan't tell any more
stories, but rather give a literal exposition. Look at it this
way; is there or is there not one quality which every citizen must have, if there is to be a city at all? On this point,   e
and this alone, depends the solution of this problem of
yours. For if there is, and this one quality isn't skill in
carpentry or in metalwork or in pottery but justice and   325a
soundness of mind and holiness—human excellence, in a
word—if this is the quality which everyone must have and
always display, whatever else he wants to learn or to do,
and anyone who lacks it, man, woman or child, must be   5
taught and punished until he reforms, and anyone who
doesn't respond to teaching and punishment must be regarded as incurable and banished from the city or put to
death—if that's the way things are, but none the less good   b
men have their sons taught other things, but not this, then
think how astonishing their behaviour is. For we have
shown that they regard it both in the private and in the   5
public sphere as something that can be taught. So though

21

it can be taught and fostered, nevertheless they have their sons taught other things, do they, where ignorance doesn't carry the death penalty, but in that sphere where their own sons must suffer death or exile if they are not taught and brought up to be good, not to mention the confiscation of their goods and in a word the absolute ruin of themselves and their families, they don't take the utmost care to have them properly taught? No, Socrates, you ought to realize that they begin when their children are small, and go on teaching and correcting them as long as they live. For as soon as a child can understand what is said to him, his nurse and his mother and his teacher and his father himself strive to make him as good as possible, teaching and showing him by every word and deed that this is right, and that wrong, this praiseworthy and that shameful, this holy and that unholy, "do this" and "don't do that". If he obeys voluntarily, so much the better; if not, they treat him like a piece of wood which is getting warped and crooked, and straighten him out with threats and beatings. And then when they send him to school they tell the teachers to pay much more attention to the children's behaviour than to their letters or their music. The teachers do that, and then when they have learned their letters and are going on to understand the written word, just as they did with speech before, they set before them at their desks the works of good poets to read, and make them learn them by heart; they contain a lot of exhortation, and many passages praising and eulogizing good men of the past, so that the child will be fired with enthusiasm to imitate them, and filled with the desire to become a man like that. The music teachers, too, do just the same, and see to it that the children are well behaved and don't do anything bad. Moreover, once they have learned to play the lyre, they teach them the poems of other good poets, lyric poets in this case, which they set to music and make the children's souls habituated to the rhythms and the melodies, so that they become gentler, more graceful, and better adjusted, and so better in word and action. For every aspect of human life requires grace and proper adjustment. And then they send them to a trainer as well, so that once their minds are properly formed their bodies will be in a better condition to act under their direction, and they won't be forced by physical deficiency to act the coward in battle or in any other situation. The people who are best able to do it—I mean, the wealthiest—do this especially, and their sons begin to go to school at the earliest age and stay there the longest. And when they have left school the city itself makes them learn the laws and live according to their example, and not just act in any way they like. Just as, when a child is still learning to write, the teacher draws lines on his book with his pencil and then makes him write the letters following the lines, so the city lays down laws, devised by good lawgivers of the past, for our guidance, and makes us rule and be ruled according to them, and punishes anyone who transgresses them. This punishment is called correction, both here and in many other cities, since the law corrects. Considering, then, that such trouble is taken about excellence both by the state and by private individuals, are you really surprised, Socrates, and doubtful that it can be taught? You ought not to be; it would be far more surprising if it could not be taught.

'Why, then, do good men often have worthless sons? The reason is this; it's not at all surprising, if it's true what I said before, that excellence is something of which no one must be ignorant, if there is to be a city at all. If, then, it's as I say—and it most certainly is—think of any pursuit or branch of knowledge that you care to take as an example. Suppose that there could not be a city unless we all played the aulos to the best of our ability, and everyone was in the habit of teaching the next man this both privately and publicly, and reproving him when he played badly, and not refusing to share his knowledge with him, just as at the moment no one refuses to share his knowledge of what is right and lawful, or conceals it, as in the case of other crafts—for we benefit, I believe, from one another's justice and goodness, which is why everyone is eager to teach the next man and tell him what

5 is right and lawful. If, then, we were all so willing and
eager to teach one another to play the aulos, do you think,
Socrates, that the sons of good aulos-players would themselves turn out to be better players than the sons of poor
players? I think not, but whoever had a son with the
c greatest natural talent for the aulos, his son would grow
up to be famous, and if anyone had a son with no talent,
he would remain unknown. And often the son of a good
player would turn out poor, and the son of a poor player
good. But all the same they would all be competent
players, compared with people who can't play at all. And
5 similarly, as things stand, you must realize that even the
wickedest man who has been brought up in a society
governed by laws is a just men, an expert in this sphere,
d if you were to compare him with men without education,
or courts, or laws, or any coercion at all to force them to
be good; they would be savages like those in the poet
5 Pherecrates'* play at last year's Lenaea. My goodness, once
you were among people of that sort, like the misanthropes
in that play, you'd be glad to fall in with Eurybatus and
Phrynondas,* and you'd weep with longing for the wicked-
e ness of people here. But now you are acting like a spoiled
child, Socrates; everybody is a teacher of excellence, to the
best of his ability, and yet you can't find anyone who is.
328a Why, just as if you were looking for a teacher of Greek,
you wouldn't find one, nor, I imagine, if you were looking
for someone to teach the sons of craftsmen the craft they
5 learn from their father, in so far as he and his friends in
the craft can teach them, would it be easy to find a teacher,
though it's perfectly easy to find someone to teach complete novices; it's just the same with excellence and all the
rest. But if there is anyone of us who is even a little better
b than others at helping people to attain it, so much the
better. I claim to be one such, and to excel others in
making people fine and good, and to be worth the fee I
5 charge and even more, as my pupils agree. For this reason
I have devised the following system of charging; whenever
c anyone has completed his study with me, if he is willing,
he pays me the fee I charge, but if not he goes to a temple,

states on oath how much he thinks what he has learnt is worth, and pays down that amount.

'So much, Socrates, by way of story and argument, to show that excellence can be taught, and that the Athenians are of that opinion, and also that it isn't at all surprising that the sons of good men turn out bad, and the sons of bad men good, since even the sons of Polycleitus, the same age as Paralus and Xanthippus here, are not to be compared with their father, and similarly in the case of other experts. But as yet it's not right to find fault with these two; one can still hope for something for them, for they are young yet.'*

328d3–329d2 Reaction of Socrates to the speech of Protagoras. He asks Protagoras whether the various virtues are distinct constituents of a total excellence, or whether they are identical with one another.

So Protagoras concluded this lengthy exhibition of his skill as a speaker. I stayed gazing at him, quite spellbound, for a long time, thinking that he was going to say something more, and anxious to hear it; but when I saw that he had really finished, I collected myself with an effort, so to speak, and looked at Hippocrates. 'Son of Apollodorus,' I said, 'I am most grateful to you for suggesting that I should come here; for what I've learnt from Protagoras is something of great importance. Previously I used to think that there was no technique available to men for making people good; but now I am persuaded that there is. I've just one small difficulty, and it's obvious that Protagoras will explain it too without any trouble, since he has explained so much already. Now if you went to any of the orators about this question, you would perhaps get a similar speech from Pericles, or from some other able speaker; but if you ask them any question, they are no more capable of answering or asking anything themselves than a book is. Ask them anything about what they've said, no matter how small a point, and just as bronze, once struck, goes on sounding for a long time until you take hold of

b   it, so these orators spin out an answer a mile long to any
little question. But Protagoras can not only give splendid
long speeches, as he has shown here, but he can also
answer questions briefly, and when he asks one himself he
5   waits and listens to the answer, which is a gift that few
possess. Now, Protagoras, I've very nearly got the whole
thing, if you would just answer me this. You say that
excellence can be taught, and I should accept your view
c   rather than anyone else's; just satisfy me on something
which surprised me when you said it. You said that Zeus
bestowed justice and conscience on mankind, and then
many times in your discourse you spoke of justice and
5   soundness of mind and holiness and all the rest as all
summed up as the one thing, excellence. Will you then
explain precisely whether excellence is one thing, and justice and soundness of mind and holiness parts of it, or
d   whether all of these that I've just mentioned are different
names of one and the same thing. This is what I still want
to know.'*

329d3–331b8 *Protagoras replies that the different virtues are distinct parts of a total excellence. Socrates gives
an argument which attempts to reduce this position to
absurdity.*

    'That's an easy question to answer, Socrates,' he said.
'Excellence is a single thing, and the things you ask about
are parts of it.'*
5   'Do you mean in the way that the parts of a face, mouth,
nose, eyes, and ears, are parts of the whole,' I asked, 'or
like parts of gold, none of which differs from any of the
others or from the whole, except in size?'
e   'The former, I take it, Socrates; the way the parts of the
face are related to the whole face.'
    'So do some people possess one of these parts of excel-
lence and some another,' I asked, 'or if someone has one,
must he have them all?'
5   'Not at all,' he said. 'There are many who are courageous but unjust, and many who are just but not wise.'

'So are wisdom and courage parts of excellence as well?' 330a
I said.

'Most certainly,' he replied. 'Wisdom is the most important part.'

'But each of them is something different from any of the
others?'

'Yes.'

'And does each of them have its own separate power?
When we consider the face, the eye is not like the ear, nor   5
is its power the same, nor is any other part like another
in power or in other ways. Is it the same with the parts
of excellence, that none is like any other, either in itself or   b
in its power? Surely it must be, if it corresponds to our
example.'

'It is so, Socrates.'

'So then,' I said, 'none of the other parts of excellence
is like knowledge, none is like justice, none like courage,   5
none like soundness of mind, and none like holiness.'

'No.'

'Well now,' I said, 'let's consider together what sort of
thing each one is. Here's the first question: is justice some-   c
thing, or not a thing at all? It seems to me that it is
something; what do you think?'

'I think so too.'

'Well, then, suppose someone asked us, "Tell me, is
that thing that you have just mentioned, justice, itself just   5
or unjust?" I should reply that it is just.* How would you
cast your vote? The same as mine, or different?'

'The same.'

'So my reply to the question would be that justice is
such as to be just; would you give the same answer?'   d

'Yes.'

'Suppose he went on to ask us, "Do you say that there
is also such a thing as holiness?" we should, I think, say
that we do.'

'Yes.'

'"And do you say that that too is something?" We
should say so, don't you agree?'

'I agree there too.'   5

27

' "And do you say that this thing is itself such as to be unholy, or such as to be holy?" I should be annoyed at the question, and say, "Watch what you say, sir; how could

e anything else be holy, if holiness itself is not to be holy?" What about you? Wouldn't you give the same answer?'

'Certainly,' he said.

'Suppose he carried on with his questioning: "Well, what was it that you were saying a moment ago? Didn't I hear

5 you correctly? You seemed to me to be saying that the parts of excellence are related to one another in such a way that none of them is like any other." I should say, "Yes, you heard the rest correctly, but you must have misheard if you think that I said that. It was Protagoras

331a who said it in answer to a question of mine." Suppose he said, "Is that right, Protagoras? Do you say that none of the parts of excellence is like any of the others? Is that your opinion?" What would you say?'

5 'I should have to agree, Socrates,' he said.

'Well, once we've agreed to that, Protagoras, how shall we deal with his next question? "So holiness is not such as to be something just, nor justice such as to be holy, but rather such as to be not holy; and holiness such as to be

b not just, and so unjust, and justice unholy?" What shall we reply? For my own part I should say both that justice is holy and holiness just; and, if you let me, I should give

5 the same answer on your behalf too, that justness is either the same thing as holiness or very similar, and above all that justice is like holiness and holiness like justice. Is that your view too, or had you rather that I didn't give that answer?'

331b8–332a4 *Protagoras objects to Socrates' argument; the discussion ends inconclusively.*

c 'It doesn't seem to me quite so simple, Socrates,' he said, 'that I should agree that justice is holy and holiness just. I think that there is a distinction to be made. But what does it matter? If you like, let us say that justice is holy and holiness just.'

'Oh, no,' I said. 'I don't want to examine any "If you like's" or "If you think so's" but rather to examine you and me. I emphasize "you and me" because I think that one can best examine the question by getting rid of any "Ifs".'

'Very well then,' he said. 'Justice resembles holiness in a way; since in fact anything resembles anything else in some way or other. There is a respect in which white resembles black, and hard soft, and all the other things that seem completely opposite to each other. We said before that the parts of the face have different powers and are not like one another. Well, in a way each one does resemble and is like the others. So by this line of argument you could prove, if you wanted to, that these too are all similar to one another. But it isn't right to call things "similar" just because they have some point of similarity, however small, nor "dissimilar" if they have some dissimilarity.'

I was astonished. 'Do you really think', I said, 'that the just and the holy have nothing more than some slight similarity to one another?'

'Not exactly,' he said, 'but then again it isn't as you seem to suppose.'

332a4–333b6 *Socrates argues that wisdom is identical with soundness of mind (sōphrosunē).**

'Well anyway,' I said, 'since you seem to find discussion of this point uncongenial, let's leave it and turn to something else that you said. Do you believe that there is such a thing as folly?'

'Yes.'

'And the very opposite of that is wisdom, is it not?'

'So it seems to me.'

'And when men act rightly and usefully, do you consider that they act sensibly* in so acting, or the opposite?'

'They act sensibly.'

'And surely it's with good sense that they act sensibly.'

'Most certainly.'

'And surely those who act wrongly act foolishly and do not act sensibly in so acting?'

'I agree.'

'So acting foolishly is the opposite of acting sensibly?'

'Yes.'

5 'And surely foolish acts are done with folly, and sensible ones with good sense?'

'I agree.'

'Now surely something done with strength is done strongly, and something done with weakness is done weakly.'

'Yes.'

'And something done with speed is done quickly, and c something with slowness, slowly.'

'Yes.'

'And something done in the same way, is done from the same, and something the opposite way from the opposite.'

'That's right.'

'Well now,' I said, 'is there such a thing as the beautiful?'

'Yes, there is.'

'And does it have any opposite except the ugly?'

'No, none.'

5 'Is there such a thing as the good?'

'There is.'

'Does it have any opposite apart from the bad?'

'No.'

'Is there such a thing as the high-pitched in sound?'

'Yes.'

'And that has no opposite apart from the low-pitched?'

'None.'

'So,' I said, 'each member of an opposition has only one opposite, not many.'

'I agree.'

d 'Well now,' I said, 'let's take a look at what we've agreed. We've agreed that each thing has only one opposite, and not more.'

'Yes, we have.'

'And that what is done in the opposite way is done from the opposite.'

'Yes.'

'And we've agreed that something done foolishly is done   5
in the opposite way to something done sensibly.'

'Yes.'

'And something done sensibly is done from good sense,
and something done foolishly from folly.'

'That is so.'   e

'Surely if it's done in the opposite way, it's done from
the opposite.'

'Yes.'

'The one is done from good sense, the other from folly.'

'Yes.'

'In opposite ways?'

'Certainly.'

'So from opposites?'

'Yes.'

'So folly is the opposite of good sense?'   5

'So it appears.'

'Now do you remember that we previously agreed that
folly is opposite to wisdom?'

'Yes, I do.'

'And that each thing has only one opposite?'

'Yes.'   333a

'Which of our theses shall we give up, then, Protagoras?
The thesis that each thing has only one opposite, or the
one that said that wisdom is distinct from good sense,
both being parts of excellence, and not only distinct but   5
dissimilar in themselves and in their powers, like the parts
of the face? Which shall we give up? For the two are not
altogether harmonious; they are not in tune, nor do they
fit together. How could they be in tune, if on the one hand
each thing must have only one opposite, and no more,   b
and on the other folly, a single thing, turns out to have
both wisdom and good sense as its opposites? Is that the
way it is, Protagoras, or not?' I asked, and he very reluc-
tantly admitted that it was.

'So good sense and wisdom would seem to be one and
the same, would they not? And previously, you recall, we   5
saw that justice and holiness were virtually the same.'

333b7–334a2 *Socrates begins an argument to prove the
identity of justice with sōphrosunē.*

'Well now, Protagoras,' I said, 'don't let's give up, but
c let's complete our inquiry. Do you think that a man who
acts unjustly is sensible in so acting?'

'I should be ashamed to assent to that, Socrates,' he
said, 'though many people say so.'

'Would you rather that I pursued the question with
them', I asked, 'or with you?'

5 'If you will,' he said, 'deal with that popular opinion
first.'

'I don't mind, provided that you answer the questions,
whether you believe the answers or not. It is chiefly the
thesis that I am testing, but all the same it perhaps turns
out to be a test for me too, as I ask the questions, and for
whoever is answering.'

d At first Protagoras began to make difficulties, saying
that it was an uncongenial thesis, but in the end he agreed
to answer the questions. 'Come then,' I said, 'answer from
the beginning. Do you agree that some people act sensibly
in acting unjustly?'

'Let's say so.'

'And by acting sensibly you mean thinking well?'

5 'Yes.'

'And by thinking well you mean planning their unjust
acts well?'

'Let's say so.'

'And do they plan well if they do well in their unjust
acts, or if they do badly?'

'If they do well.'

'Do you call some things good?'

'I do.'

'Now,' I said, 'are those things good which are beneficial to people?'

e 'My goodness, yes,' he said, 'and there are things I call
good even though they aren't beneficial to people.'

I could see that Protagoras was annoyed by this time,
and that he was ready for a verbal battle and keen to get

to grips; so when I saw that, I took care to put my questions in a mild manner. 'Do you mean things that aren't beneficial to any human being, Protagoras,' I asked, 'or 334a things that aren't beneficial at all? Do you call things like that good too?'

334a3–c6 *Protagoras interrupts the argument with a short speech on the complexity and relational nature of goodness.*

'Not at all,' he said. 'I know of many things which are harmful to humans, food and drink and drugs and a thousand other things, and of some which are beneficial. Some things have neither effect on humans, but have an effect on horses; some have no effect except on cattle, or on dogs. Some have no effect on any animal, but do affect trees. And some things are good for the roots of the tree, but bad for the growing parts, for instance manure is b good if applied to the roots of all plants, but if you put it on the shoots and young twigs it destroys everything. Oil, too, is very bad for all plants and most destructive of the hair of animals other than man, but in the case of man 5 it is beneficial to the hair and to the rest of the body. So varied and many-sided a thing is goodness, that even here the very same thing is good for the outside of the human c body, and very bad for the inside. That is the reason why doctors all forbid sick people to use oil in their food except in the smallest quantities, just enough to cover up 5 any unpleasant smell from the dishes and garnishes.'*

334c7–335c7 *Socrates protests at the length of Protagoras' speech and makes as if to break off the discussion.*

When he had finished the audience shouted their approval of his speech, and I said, 'Protagoras, I happen to be a forgetful sort of person, and if someone speaks to me at d length, I forget what he is talking about. It's just as if I were a trifle deaf; in that case you would think it right to speak louder than usual, if you were going to talk to me.

So now, since you are dealing with someone with a bad
5   memory, cut your answers short and make them briefer,
if I am to follow you.'

'What do you mean by telling me to give short answers?' he asked. 'Are they to be shorter than the questions require?'

'By no means,' I said.

'The right length, then?'

e   'Yes.'

'So are they to be the length that I think right, or that
you do?'

5   'Well, I've heard', I said, 'that you can speak at such
length, when you choose to, that your speech never comes
335a to an end, and then again you can be so brief on the same
topic that no one could be briefer, and as well as doing it
yourself you can teach someone else how to do it. So if
you are going to have a discussion with me, use the latter
method, that of brevity.'

'Socrates,' he said, 'I've had verbal contests with a great
5   many people, and if I had done what you tell me to do,
and spoken according to the instructions of my antagonist, I should never have got the better of anyone, nor
would the name of Protagoras have become known in
Greece.'*

b   I knew that he was dissatisfied with his previous replies,
and that he wasn't willing to take the role of answerer in
the discussion, so I felt that there was no point in my
5   continuing the conversation. 'Well, Protagoras,' I said, 'I
too am not happy about carrying on the conversation in
a way that is unacceptable to you. But whenever you wish
to have a discussion of the kind that I can follow, then I
shall take part with you. You can carry on a conversation,
so they say, and indeed you say so yourself, either by long
c   speeches or by short question and answer—you are such
an able man—but I can't make these long speeches, though
I wish I could. As you can argue in both styles, you should
have made me some concession, so that we could have
had a conversation. But now, since you are not willing to
5   do so, and I have an engagement, and couldn't wait for

you to spin out these long speeches—I have to go some-
where—I shall go. Though I should no doubt have been
glad to hear what you have to say.'

335c8–338e5 *Argument as to how the discussion should
be continued. It is agreed to proceed by question and
answer, with Protagoras questioning first.*

At the same time I got up to go. And as I was getting up
Callias grasped my hand in his right hand, and with his   d
left took hold of this old cloak of mine, and said, 'We
shan't let you go, Socrates; for if you leave, our discussion
won't be the same. So I beg you to stay with us; there's
nothing I'd rather listen to than a discussion between you
and Protagoras. Please oblige us all.'   5
    By this time I had got up to go. 'Son of Hipponicus,' I
said, 'I've always had a high regard for your love of learn- e
ing, but now I praise and love it, so that I should like to
oblige you, if you asked me something possible. But now
it's as if you were asking me to keep pace with Crison,*
the runner from Himera, at his peak, or keep up in a race
with some middle-distance runner or long-distance courier.* I should reply that I am far more eager than you to 336a
keep pace with them, but I can't, so if you want to watch
Crison and me running together, ask him to come down
to my level; for I can't run fast, but he can run slowly. So   5
if you want to listen to Protagoras and me, ask him to
answer now the way he did at first, briefly, and sticking
to the question. If not, what sort of discussion will we   b
have? I thought that a discussion was something quite
different from a public speech.'
    'But, you see, Socrates,' he said, 'Protagoras seems quite
right in asking to be allowed to speak as he likes, and for   5
you to speak as you like.'
    Alcibiades broke in; 'That's not fair, Callias. Socrates
admits that he doesn't go in for speech-making, and con-
cedes victory in that sphere to Protagoras, but when it   c
comes to discussion and ability to handle question and
answer, I should be surprised if he yields to anyone. So if

Protagoras admits that he is inferior to Socrates in discussion, Socrates is content; but if he disputes it, let him conduct a discussion by question and answer, and not make a long speech in reply to every question, staving off objections and not giving answers, but spinning it out until most of the people listening forget what the question was. Except Socrates, of course; I bet that he won't forget, but he's only joking when he says he has a bad memory. I think, then, that what Socrates says is fairer; and each of us ought to give his own opinion.'

After Alcibiades, I think it was Critias who spoke. 'Prodicus and Hippias, Callias seems to me very much on the side of Protagoras, while Alcibiades takes a partisan view of anything he is keen on. But there is no reason for us to take sides either with Socrates or with Protagoras; instead we should ask both of them not to break off the conversation in the middle.'

Then Prodicus said, 'I agree, Critias. Those who attend a discussion like this should listen to both speakers impartially, but not without discrimination—that's not the same thing. For one ought to listen to both impartially, while not assessing each equally, but putting the abler man above the less able. For my own part, Socrates and Protagoras, I think that you should agree to argue, but not wrangle—for an argument can be between friends in a spirit of good will, a wrangle is between those who are hostile and unfriendly to one another—and so we should have a splendid conversation. For in that way you who speak would gain the most esteem, though not praise, from us who listen—for esteem is something genuine in the minds of one's hearers, while praise is often mere deceitful words contrary to their real opinion—while we who listen would derive in that way the most enjoyment, though not pleasure —for one derives enjoyment from learning and the exercise of intelligence purely in the mind, but pleasure from eating or some other pleasant experience purely in the body.'*

Very many of those present agreed with these remarks of Prodicus'. And then the wise Hippias said, 'Gentlemen,

I regard you as all related, all akin, all fellow citizens—by   d
nature, not by convention. For like is by nature akin to
like, but convention, a tyrant over mankind, ordains many
things by force contrary to nature.* Surely, therefore, it is
shameful if we, who understand the nature of things and,   5
being the wisest of the Greeks, have for that very reason
come together to the very shrine of wisdom in all Greece
and to this, the greatest and most magnificent house of
that very city, should achieve nothing worthy of our repu-   e
tation, but quarrel among ourselves like the most worthless of people. I beg and counsel you then, Protagoras and
Socrates, to regard us as arbitrators and come to an agree-   338a
ment. For your part, Socrates, I advise you not to seek that
sort of precision in the discussion which involves excessive
brevity, if that is not agreeable to Protagoras, but to let go
and slacken the reins of the discourse, so as to give it
more dignity and elegance. And on the other hand I advise   5
Protagoras not to crowd on all sail and run before the
wind into a sea of words out of sight of land; both of you
should take a middle course. So do as I suggest, and choose
an umpire, chairman, or president to see that each of you   b
keeps to the proper length in what he says.'

This was agreeable to the company; everyone indicated
his approval, and Callias refused to let me go and they
asked me to choose a chairman. I then said that it was
quite improper to choose a referee for an argument. 'For   5
if the person chosen is inferior to ourselves,' I said, 'it
would not be right for an inferior person to preside over
men better than he, and if he is our equal, even then it
wouldn't be right; for someone who is our equal will do
just the same as we should, so it will be a waste of time   c
to choose him. All right, then, you will choose someone
superior to us. But in fact I think that it's impossible to
choose anyone wiser than Protagoras. And if you choose
someone who is in no way superior, while pretending that
he is, then that too is an insult to Protagoras, to have a
chairman chosen for him as if he were of no account. As   5
far as I am concerned, it makes no difference. But here's
what I am willing to do, so that we can have a discussion

as you are anxious to do. If Protagoras is not willing to
d   answer, let him put the questions, and I shall answer, and
at the same time I shall try to show him how, in my
opinion, one ought to answer questions. And when I have
5   answered all the questions he wants to ask, let him in turn
undergo questioning from me in the same way. So if he
doesn't seem anxious to stick to the question in his replies, you and I together will ask him, as you asked me,
e   not to ruin the conversation. There's no need for any
single chairman to be appointed for that; instead you will
all act together as chairmen.'

Everyone agreed that that was what we should do.
Protagoras was altogether unwilling, but none the less he
5   was obliged to agree to put the questions, and when he
had asked sufficient, to submit to questioning in his turn
and give short replies.

338e6–347a5   *The discussion is continued by means of
the criticism of a poem of Simonides, first by Protagoras
and then by Socrates.*

So he began to put his questions something like this: 'I
consider, Socrates, that a most important part of a man's
339a education is being knowledgeable about poetry. By that I
mean the ability to grasp the good and bad points of a
poem, to distinguish them and to give one's reasons in
5   reply to questions.* And in fact the question that I am now
going to ask concerns the very thing we are discussing
now, excellence; the only difference is that it is transferred
to the sphere of poetry. Simonides in one of his poems
says to Scopas the son of Creon of Thessaly that

b   It is hard, rather, to become a truly good man,
            Foursquare in hand and foot and mind, fashioned
                without fault.

Do you know this poem, or shall I recite it all for you?'
5   'There's no need,' I said. 'I know it, and as it happens
I've studied it closely.'

38

'Good,' he said. 'Do you regard it as a fine, properly written poem, or not?'

'Very fine and properly written.'

'Do you count it a fine poem, if the poet contradicts   10
himself?'

'No.'

'Then look at it more closely.'   c

'But, my dear sir, I have studied it sufficiently already.'

'You know, then, that later on in the poem he says

> Nor do I hold as right the saying of Pittacus,*
> Wise though he was; he says it is hard to be noble.   5

Do you think it is the same man who says that and the lines I quoted earlier?'

'I know that it is.'

'You think, then, that the two are consistent?'

'Personally, I do,' I said (though at the same time I was afraid he might be right). 'Don't you?'

'But how could anyone be thought to be consistent in   d
saying both these things? First of all he himself asserts that it is hard to become a truly good man, and then a little further on he forgets that and attacks Pittacus for   5
saying just what he has said, that it is hard to be noble, and refuses to accept it, though it's the same as his own view. But in attacking someone for saying just what he says, he is obviously attacking himself, so either the earlier or the later statement must be wrong.'

This produced a shout of approval from many of the   10
audience. At first, what with his argument and the ap-   e
plause of the others, my eyes went dim and I felt giddy, as if I had been hit by a good boxer. But then—to tell you the truth, it was to gain time to consider what the poet meant—I turned to Prodicus and addressed him. 'Prodicus,   5
Simonides is a fellow citizen* of yours; you ought to come 340a
to his assistance. So now I'm resolved to call on you for help. Just as Homer says Scamander called on Simoeis for help when he was attacked by Achilles, in these words,

> Dear brother, let both of us restrain the man's strength,*   5

39

so I call on you to help stop Protagoras utterly demolishing Simonides. And certainly the defence of Simonides requires your special skill, which enables you to distinguish wishing from desiring, and all those splendid distinctions you made a short time ago. Now see whether you agree with me. For Simonides doesn't seem to me to contradict himself. But please give your opinion first, Prodicus; do you think that becoming and being are the same thing, or different?'

'Different, of course.'

'Now in the first passage doesn't Simonides give his own opinion, that it is hard to become a truly good man?'

'That's correct.'

'But he attacks Pittacus,' I said, 'not, as Protagoras thinks, for saying the same as he does, but for saying something different. For it's not *becoming* noble that Pittacus says is difficult, as Simonides does, but *being* noble. And as Prodicus says, Protagoras, being and becoming are not the same thing. And if being is not the same as becoming, Simonides does not contradict himself. Perhaps Prodicus and many others would say in the words of Hesiod that it is difficult to become good,

For the gods have placed sweat on the path to excellence,

But when you reach the top,

Thereafter it is easy to keep, hard though it was to achieve.'*

Prodicus indicated his agreement, but Protagoras said, 'Your defence, Socrates, involves a worse mistake than the one you are defending him against.'

'Well then, Protagoras, it seems I've done harm,' I said, 'and I'm a ridiculous sort of doctor, for my treatment makes the disease worse.'

'Well, that's the way it is.'

'How do you mean?'

'It would show great stupidity on the poet's part if he says that it is so easy to keep excellence once you have it, when that's the most difficult thing of all, as everyone agrees.'

'My goodness,' I said, 'it's lucky that we have Prodicus taking part in our discussion. You know, Protagoras, that 341a skill of his must be a marvellous and ancient one, originating with Simonides, or even earlier. But though you are learned in so many other things, you don't seem to be acquainted with it, as I am through being Prodicus' pupil. And in the present case you don't seem to me to see that 5 by "hard" Simonides perhaps didn't mean what you mean. It's like "terrible"; whenever I say in praise of you or anyone else that Protagoras is a terribly wise man, Prodicus corrects me and asks if I'm not ashamed to call something b good terrible. For what is terrible, he says, is bad; at least no one ever talks of "terrible wealth" or "terrible peace" or "terrible health", but "terrible disease" and "terrible war" 5 and "terrible poverty", which shows that what is terrible is bad. So perhaps it's the same with "hard"; perhaps Simonides and the Ceans use it in the sense of "bad", or some other sense which you haven't grasped. So let's ask Prodicus; it's reasonable to ask him about Simonides' dia- c lect. What did Simonides mean by "hard", Prodicus?'

'"Bad"' he replied.

'So that's the reason', I said, 'why he attacks Pittacus for saying "It is hard to be noble", as if he had heard him 5 saying "It is bad to be noble".'

'You surely don't imagine, Socrates,' he said, 'that Simonides means anything else. He is censuring Pittacus for not distinguishing the sense of words correctly, coming from Lesbos as he did and having been brought up to speak a foreign language.'

'Well, Protagoras,' I said, 'you hear what Prodicus says. 10 Have you anything to say to that?' d

'It's not that way at all, Prodicus,' answered Protagoras. 'I know perfectly well that by "hard" Simonides means what we all mean, not "bad" but what is not easy, and 5 can't be attained without a great deal of trouble.'

'Well I think so too, Protagoras,' I said. 'That's what Simonides means, and Prodicus knows it as well, but he's having a joke and testing you to see whether you can defend your position. That Simonides doesn't mean "bad"

e   by "hard" is shown quite clearly by what he says immediately afterwards. He says

> That gift would belong to a god alone.

Now clearly he isn't saying "It is bad to be noble", and
5   then going on to say that the gods alone would possess
that gift, and to assign it to them alone. Prodicus would
be making Simonides out to be some sort of scoundrel,
never a Cean.* But I am willing to tell you what I think
342a Simonides means in this poem, if you want to have a
sample of my knowledge of poetry, as you call it. Or if
you like, I shall listen to your explanation.'

When I had finished Protagoras said, 'If *you* like, Soc-
5   rates.' Prodicus and Hippias told me to go ahead by all
means, and so did the others.

'Well,' I said, 'I shall try to explain my own view of this
poem. The most ancient learning of Greece, and the most
copious, is to be found in Crete and in Sparta,* and there
b   are more wise men* there than anywhere else on earth.
But they deny this and pretend to be ignorant, so as not to
betray their superiority in wisdom over the rest of Greece,
like those whom Protagoras described as sophists. Instead,
they try to make it look as if they excel in courage and in
5   fighting, for they think that if their real superiority were
discovered, everyone would seek to acquire wisdom. Up
to the present they have concealed this and deceived their
c   admirers in other cities, who imitate them by putting on
boxing-gloves, getting cauliflower ears, going in for gym-
nastics and wearing short cloaks, in the belief that those
are the things that make the Spartans superior to other
5   Greeks. But the Spartans themselves, whenever they get
tired of concealment and want to consult their wise men
openly, expel any foreigners, those admirers of theirs as
well as anyone else who happens to be in the country, and
so consult the wise men unknown to foreigners; and they
d   don't allow any of their young men to go abroad, and
neither do the Cretans, to make sure they don't forget
what they are taught at home. And in those cities you find
not only men who take pride in their education, but women

too. This is how you'll see that what I say is true, that the
Spartans have the best education and the greatest skill   5
with words: if you meet the most ordinary Spartan, for
most of the conversation he strikes you as a dull fellow,   e
and then, no matter what you are talking about, he flings in
some memorable, brief, pithy saying like a skilful javelin-
thrower, making the man he is talking to look no more
than a child. Now there are some, both of earlier times   5
and of our own day, who have seen that admiration of
Sparta is much more a matter of learning than of gymnas-
tics, and who know that the ability to utter sayings of 343a
that kind is the mark of a perfectly educated man. Thales
of Miletus was one, Pittacus of Mytilene another, Bias of
Priene, our own Solon, Cleobulus of Lindos, Myson of
Chen(ae); the Spartan Chilon was counted as the seventh.   5
All of these were admirers, devotees, and students of the
Spartan education, and you can see that their own wisdom is of that kind, as each is the author of some brief,
memorable sayings. And not only that, but they joined   b
together to make an offering to Apollo at his temple in
Delphi of the fruits of their wisdom, and inscribed there
those familiar maxims "Know thyself" and "Nothing in
excess".* What, then, is the point of all this? The point is
that that was the form of expression of the wisdom of
former times, a Laconian brevity. And one of Pittacus'   3
sayings which circulated privately and won the approval
of the wise was this one, "It is hard to be good." So
Simonides, who was anxious to get a reputation for wis-   c
dom, saw that if he could bring down that saying then,
just as if he had defeated a famous athlete, he would
himself become famous among the men of his time. That
was his object, I believe, and it is that saying that he has
in mind throughout the whole poem, with the aim of   5
discrediting it.

'Let's all examine it together, then, to see whether what
I say is true. For right away the beginning of the poem
would seem quite crazy, if he wanted to say that it is hard
to become a good man, and then added "rather". For that   d
phrase does not seem to have been added for any purpose,

43

unless one understands Simonides as arguing against the saying of Pittacus. When Pittacus says that it is hard to be

5 noble, Simonides replies, "No, but rather to *become* a good man, Pittacus, is hard in truth"—he doesn't say "a truly good man", or apply truth to that, as if there were

e some men who are truly good, and others who are good indeed, but not truly so (that would strike people as silly and not something that Simonides would say). You have to take the phrase "in truth" as transposed in the poem, and as it were prefix the saying of Pittacus, as if we were

5 to imagine Pittacus himself speaking and Simonides replying, thus: "It is hard to be noble", (Simonides in reply)

344a "Pittacus, what you are saying is not true: for it is not to *be*, but rather to *become* a good man, foursquare in hand and foot and mind, fashioned without fault, that is hard

5 in truth." Taken like that, "rather" appears to have been added for some purpose, and "in truth" put in its proper place at the end; and everything that follows supports that way of taking it. Now there are many things which one could say about each of the expressions in the poem to

b show that it is well written—for it is a quite delightful, carefully composed work—but it would take a long time to go through it like that. Let's just examine the outline of the piece as a whole and its intention, which is above

5 all to criticize the saying of Pittacus throughout the poem.

'For a little later, as if he were developing his argument, he says that to become a good man is truly difficult, but

c possible, for a time at least; but having become one, to remain in that state and be a good man, as you say, Pittacus, is impossible and beyond human power, but only a god could have that gift.

> And it is impossible for the man not to be bad,
5 > Whom helpless disaster overthrows.

Now in controlling a ship, who is it whom helpless disaster overthrows? Clearly not the man without knowledge of sailing; for he has been overthrown from the start. So just as you can't throw a man who is already down, but you can throw a man who is on his feet, and put him down,

but not if he's down already, similarly helpless disaster   d
can sometimes overthrow the resourceful man, but not the
man who is always helpless, and a helmsman can be struck
and rendered helpless by a great storm, and a farmer made
helpless by the onset of a bad season, and the same with
a doctor. For the noble man can become bad, as we learn   5
from another poet who says

Now a good man is sometimes bad and sometimes noble;

but the bad man can't become bad, but must always be   e
so. So when helpless disaster overthrows the resourceful,
wise, and good man, it is impossible for him not to be
bad. But you, Pittacus, say that it is hard to be noble; but
in fact to become noble is hard, but possible, but to be   5
noble is impossible,

> For when he does well every man is good,
> But bad when he does badly.

Now as regards reading and writing, what counts as do-   345a
ing well, and what kind of doing makes a man good at
that? Obviously, having learned his letters. And what is
the doing well that makes a man a good doctor? Obviously, having learned how to care for the sick. "But bad
when he does badly." Now who could become a bad   5
doctor? Obviously, someone who is first of all a doctor,
and then a good doctor—for he is the man who could
become bad—but the rest of us who are ignorant of
medicine could never in doing badly become doctors or   b
carpenters or anything else of the kind; and someone who
could never in doing badly become a doctor could obviously not become a bad doctor either. So it is that the
good man too could sometimes become bad, either through
age or toil or disease or some misfortune—for doing badly   5
is nothing other than being deprived of knowledge—but
the bad man could never become bad—for he is bad all
the time—but if he is to become bad he must first become
good. So this part of the poem too points to the same
conclusion, that it is impossible to be a good man, good   c
all the time, that is, but it is possible to become good and

for the same man to become bad. And the best, who are good for longest, are those whom the gods love.

5   'So all of this was written against Pittacus, and the next section of the poem shows that even more clearly. For he says

Therefore never shall I cast empty away my share of time
On a vain hope, seeking what cannot be, an utterly blameless
10   Man, of us who reap the fruit of broad earth,
And when I find him, I shall tell you,

d   he says—so fierce is his attack on Pittacus' maxim throughout the poem—

        But I praise and love all
        Who do nothing shameful freely;
5   But against necessity not even gods fight.

And this too was directed at the same target. For Simonides was not so uneducated as to say he praised those who do nothing bad of their own free will, as if there were some
e   people who do bad things freely. For I am pretty much of this opinion, that no intelligent man believes that anyone does wrong freely or acts shamefully and badly of his own free will, but they well know that all who do shameful and bad things do so other than freely.* And Simonides,
5   for his part, doesn't say that he praises those who do nothing bad freely, but he applies this term "freely" to himself. For he thought that an honest man often forces
346a himself to be a friend and praise someone; for instance, it often happens that a man has an unnatural father or mother, or country, or something like that. When that happens to a bad man he views it almost with pleasure
5   and makes a great display of castigating and blaming the shortcomings of his parents or his country, in order that he himself may not incur any blame or reproach for his neglect of them, so he berates them even more than need
b   be, and deliberately makes new enemies on top of those he can't avoid. But a good man conceals it all and forces himself to praise them, and if he gets angry at his unjust treatment by his parents or his country he calms himself

down and makes friends again, forcing himself to love   5
and praise them.

'Often, I think, Simonides considered that he himself
was praising and eulogizing a tyrant or someone else, not
freely, but under compulsion. It is this that he has in mind
when he says to Pittacus, "For my part, Pittacus, it's not
because I am a fault-finder that I censure you, since   c

> He suffices me who is not bad nor
> Altogether wicked, a sound man who knows
> Justice that benefits the city.   5
> Him I shall not censure—

for I am not one who loves to censure—

> For the generation of fools is endless.

(So if anyone likes finding fault, he could have his fill on   10
them.)

> Now all things are fair, which are not mingled with foul."

When he says that, it's not as if he were saying "All things   d
are white, which are not mingled with black"—that would
be absurd for many reasons—but that he himself accepts
the middle state as free from censure. "I do not seek", he
says, "an utterly blameless man, of us who reap the fruit   5
of broad earth, and when I find him I shall tell you. So I
shan't praise anyone for being such a man; it is enough
for me if he is in between and does nothing bad, for I
praise and love all"—and here he uses the Mytilenean
dialect, since it is against Pittacus that he says, "I praise   e
and love all freely"—it's there, at "freely", that one must
divide the phrase—"who do nothing shameful, but there
are some whom I praise and love against my will. So if
you, Pittacus, said what was even partly right and true, I 347a
should never find fault with you. But since you give the
appearance of speaking the truth when in fact you are
totally wrong on things of the greatest importance, for
that reason I blame you." That, gentlemen,' I said, 'is
what Simonides seems to me to have meant in writing this   5
poem.'

47

347a6–348c4 *It is agreed to abandon criticism of poetry and to resume the original discussion.*

b 'Socrates,' replied Hippias, 'you too seem to me to have given a good account of the poem. I, too, though, have a good interpretation of it, which I shall expound to you all, if you like.'

'Yes, Hippias,' said Alcibiades, 'some other time. But now it's right that Protagoras and Socrates should honour their agreement, and if Protagoras wants to ask any more questions, Socrates should answer, or if Protagoras wants to answer, Socrates should ask the questions.'

And I said, 'For my part, I concede to Protagoras which-ever he prefers; and if he is willing, let's leave the discus-

c sion of lyric and other kinds of poetry, but I should be very glad, Protagoras, to complete our examination of the question I asked you at first. For the discussion of poetry strikes me as very like a drinking-party of common, vul-

5 gar fellows; for people of that sort, who for lack of edu-cation can't entertain one another over the wine with their

d own conversation, put up the price of musicians, and pay large sums to hear the sound of the aulos instead of their own talk, and entertain each other that way. But in a party of well-bred, educated people, you never see dancing-

5 girls, or girls playing the aulos or the harp, but they can entertain one another with their own conversation with-out any such childish trifles, speaking and listening in turn in a dignified fashion, even if they drink a great deal.

e Similarly gatherings of this kind, if they are made up of the sort of men that most of us claim to be, have no need of anyone else to take part and in particular no need of poets; you can't question them about what they say, but

5 in most cases when people quote them, one says the poet means one thing and one another, and they argue over points which can't be established with any certainty.* No,

348a they leave that kind of conversation alone, and entertain one another by their own efforts and test each other's mettle in mutual argument. It seems to me that you and I should rather follow the example of that sort of person,

48

leave the poets aside and conduct our argument independ-   5
ently, testing the truth of the matter and our own capa-
cities. And if you want to carry on asking the questions,
I'm prepared to reply; but if you're willing, oblige me
by completing the discussion which we broke off in the
middle.'

In reply to this and similar things Protagoras gave no   b
clear indication of which he was going to do. So Alcibiades
looked at Callias and said, 'Callias, do you think that Protagoras is being fair now, not telling us whether he'll answer   5
or not? I don't think so, anyhow. So let him either join in
the discussion or tell us that he's not willing to, so that we
know where he stands, and Socrates, or anyone else who
wants to, can take up a discussion with someone else.'

And Protagoras, shamed, so it seemed to me, by these   c
words of Alcibiades and by the entreaties of Callias and
practically everybody else, was at length induced to take
part, and told me to put the questions and he would
answer.

348c5–349d8 *Socrates recapitulates the initial question
and asks Protagoras for his present position. Protagoras answers that while wisdom, sōphrosunē, justice, and holiness are very much alike, courage is something completely
different.*

Then I said, 'Protagoras, please don't think that I have   5
any other aim in our discussion than to get to the bottom
of the problems that always puzzle me. For I think that
Homer certainly has a point when he talks of

Two going together, and one noticed it before the other.*   d

For somehow we all do better that way, whatever has to
be done or said or thought out. "And if he notices it
alone", he immediately goes about looking for someone   5
to show it to, to find confirmation, and doesn't stop till he
finds someone. It's for just this reason that I had rather
have a discussion with you than with anyone else, for I
think that you are best able to examine the questions that   e

49

it is right for an upright man to consider, especially questions about excellence. For who other than yourself? It's not just that you regard yourself as a worthy man; others are upright themselves without the ability to make others so. You are both good yourself and capable of making others good, and have such self-confidence that, whereas others make a secret of this profession, you give yourself the name of sophist and proclaim yourself openly to the whole of Greece as a teacher of culture and excellence, and have been the first to ask a fee for this. So should I not have called on you to explore these matters and consulted and questioned you? Of course I should. And now, with regard to my original question, I should like you to remind me once again from the beginning of what we said, and also to examine some further points together with me. The question, I think, was this: are "wisdom", "soundness of mind", "courage", "justice", and "holiness" five names for the one thing, or does there correspond to each of these names some separate thing or entity with its own particular power, unlike any of the others? Now you said that they are not names for the one thing, but each is the name of a separate thing, and all of these are parts of excellence, not as the parts of gold are like one another and the whole of which they are parts, but as the parts of the face are unlike one another and the whole of which they are parts, each having its own separate power. If you still think now as you did then, please say so; but if at all differently, please explain how, since I shan't hold you to anything if you've now changed your mind in any way. For I shouldn't be surprised if you were saying that then just to test me out.'

'Well, Socrates,' he said, 'I maintain that all of these are parts of excellence, and four of them resemble one another fairly closely, but courage is altogether different from all the rest. And this is how you will know that what I say is true: you will find many men who are totally unjust and irreligious and wanton and ignorant, but most outstandingly courageous.'

349e1–350c5 *Socrates gives an argument designed to prove that courage is identical with wisdom.**

'Stop there,' I said; 'it's worth taking a look at what   e
you are saying. Do you call courageous men daring or
something else?'

'Yes, daring,' he said, 'and ready for what most men
fear.'

'Tell me then, do you regard excellence as something
fine, and is it as something fine that you offer to teach it?'   5

'The finest of all things, unless I'm quite mad.'

'Is part of it shameful, and part fine, or is it all fine?'

'It's all as fine as anything can be.'

'Now, do you know who it is who are daring at diving 350a
into wells?'

'Yes, divers.'

'Because of their knowledge, or something else?'

'Because of their knowledge.'

'And who are daring at fighting on horseback? Cavalrymen, or people who can't ride?'

'Cavalrymen.'

'And in skirmishing? Is it trained skirmishers, or un-   5
trained?'

'Trained skirmishers,' he said. 'And in every other case,
if this is the answer you are looking for, those who have
knowledge are more daring than those who lack it, and   b
once they have acquired it they are more daring than they
themselves were before.'

'And have you ever', I asked, 'seen people who are
ignorant of all these things, but daring in each of them?'

'I have,' he said. 'Too daring.'

'So, are these daring men courageous as well?'

'In that case courage would be something shameful; for   5
such people are mad.'

'Well now, what do you say about the courageous?
Isn't it that they are (the) daring?'

'Yes, I stick to that.'

'So these people who are daring in that way seem not   c

51

courageous but mad, isn't that so? And on the other hand these people who are wisest are also most daring, and being most daring are most courageous? And according to
5   this argument wisdom would be the same as courage?'

350c6–351b2 Protagoras objects to Socrates' argument and attempts to show a fallacy in it.

'You are not correctly recalling,' he said, 'what I said in answer to your question, Socrates. You asked me if the courageous are daring, and I agreed that they are; but you didn't ask me if, in addition, the daring are courageous— for if you had asked me that, I should have said that not
d   all are. You have nowhere shown that I was wrong in what I did agree, viz. that the courageous are daring. Then you show that people when they have knowledge are more daring than when they lack it, and also than
5   others who are ignorant, and on that basis you conclude that courage and wisdom are the same thing; but if you go about it that way you might think that strength is the same thing as wisdom. For if you proceeded that way and
e   began by asking me if the strong are capable, I should say yes; and then, if those who know how to wrestle are more capable than those who don't know how to wrestle, and themselves more capable after they have learnt than before, I should say yes; and once I had agreed to that you
5   would be able, using the very same arguments, to conclude that according to what I had agreed wisdom was the same thing as strength. But I neither here nor anywhere else admit that the capable are strong, but rather that the
351a strong are capable; for capability and strength are not the same thing, but the former comes from knowledge indeed, but also from madness and animal boldness, while strength results from a good natural condition and nurture of the
5   body. And similarly in the other case daring and courage are not the same, so that it happens that the courageous are daring, but that not all the daring are courageous. For
b   daring results both from skill and from animal boldness and madness, like capability, but courage from a good natural condition and nurture of the soul.'

52

351b3–e11   *Socrates breaks off the discussion of wisdom
and courage to introduce a thesis to the effect that pleasure is in itself something (? the supreme, ? the only) good.
It is agreed to examine this thesis.**

'And do you maintain, Protagoras,' I said, 'that some
people live well and others badly?'

'I do.'

'Well, now, do you think someone would live well if he   5
lived in misery and suffering?'

'No.'

'And what if he had a pleasant life to the end? Don't
you think that he would have lived well like that?'

'Yes, I do.'

'So to have a pleasant life is good, and to have an   c
unpleasant life bad?'

'Provided one takes pleasure in praiseworthy things.'

'What's that, Protagoras? Surely you don't go along
with the majority in calling some pleasant things bad and
some painful things good. What I say is, in so far as things
are pleasant, are they not to that extent good, leaving   5
their other consequences out of account? And again it's
the same with painful things; in so far as they are painful,
are they not bad?'

'I don't know, Socrates,' he replied, 'whether I should
give such a simple answer to your question and say that   d
all pleasant things are good and all painful things bad.
Rather it seems to me safer, having regard not only to
what I say now but also to all the rest of my life, to reply
that some pleasant things are not good, and again that   5
some painful things are not bad, while some are, and a
third class is neutral, neither good nor bad.'

'And don't you call pleasant', I said, 'things which are   e
characterized by pleasure or which produce pleasure?'

'Certainly.'

'Well, that's what I'm saying; in so far as they are pleasant, are they not good? I'm asking whether pleasure itself
is not good.'

'As you always say, Socrates,' he replied, 'let's investigate

5   it. And if the question seems to the point and it appears that pleasant and good are the same, then we shall be in agreement. But if not, we shall argue about it then.'

'Do you wish to lead the investigation,' I asked, 'or shall I?'

10   'You ought to,' he said, 'as it's you who are in charge of the discussion.'

352a1–357e8 Socrates states his thesis that if one knows what is the right thing to do one necessarily does it, and defends this thesis against the common man's objection that people frequently know what to do but fail to do it because they are overcome by pleasure or other appetitive forces. He argues that the common man's hedonistic assumptions oblige him to admit that the man whom he describes as overcome by such forces is in fact led astray by error in his calculation of the consequences of his actions.

352a   'Well, then,' I said, 'perhaps things might become clear if we go about it like this. Imagine someone looking at a man and trying to assess his health or some other bodily function from his appearance, and saying, once he had

5   seen his face and hands, "Come now, uncover your chest and back and let me see them, so that I can examine you more thoroughly." I too want something of the sort as regards our question. I've seen that your view about the good and the pleasant is as you say, and now I want to

b   say something like this: "Come now, Protagoras, uncover for me this part of your mind as well; how do you stand as regards knowledge? Do you agree with the majority there too, or do you think otherwise? The opinion of the majority about knowledge is that it is not anything strong, which controls and rules; they don't look at it that way at

5   all, but think that often someone who possesses knowledge is ruled not by it but by something else, in one case passion, in another pleasure, in another pain, sometimes

c   lust, very often fear; they just look at knowledge as a slave who gets dragged about by all the rest. Now are you of a similar opinion about knowledge, or do you think

that it is something fine and such as to rule man, and that
if someone knows what is good and bad, he would never   5
be conquered by anything so as to do other than what
knowledge bids him? In fact, that intelligence is a sufficient safeguard for man?"'

'My opinion is indeed as you say, Socrates,' he replied,
'and moreover it would be an especial disgrace to me of   d
all people not to maintain that wisdom and knowledge is
the mightiest of human things.'

'That's splendid,' I said, 'and quite true. Now you know   5
that the majority of people don't agree with us, but hold
that many people who know what is best to do are not
willing to do it, though it is in their power, but do something else. And those whom I've asked about the cause of
this say that people who act in that way do so because
they are overcome by pleasure or pain or under the influ-   e
ence of one of the things I mentioned just now.'

'Yes, Socrates,' he said, 'people have many other wrong
ideas too.'

'Join me, then, in trying to win them over and to teach   5
them the real nature of the experience that they call being
overcome by pleasures and for that reason failing to do   353a
what is best, when one knows what it is. For perhaps if
we told them that they are wrong and mistaken they would
ask, "Well, if this experience isn't being overcome by pleas- 5
ure, what is it then? What do you call it? Tell us."'

'But why, Socrates, must we examine the opinion of the
mass of people, who say whatever comes into their heads?'

'I think', I replied, 'that this is relevant to our question   b
of how courage is related to the other parts of excellence.
So if you are willing to abide by what we just agreed, that
I should conduct the discussion in the way that I think   *
best suited to make the matter clear, please follow my   5
lead. But if not, if you had rather, I'll let the matter go.'

'You're quite right,' he said. 'Go on as you've begun.'

'Well once again,' I said, 'if they asked us, "What then   c
do you say this thing is, which we were calling being
weaker than pleasures?" I should answer as follows: "Listen, and Protagoras and I shall try to explain. Don't you

5 maintain that it happens that in some circumstances, often for instance when you are conquered by the pleasures of food and drink and sex, you do things though you know them to be wrong?" "Yes." So we in our turn should ask,

d "In what respect do you say they are wrong? Is it because they provide this immediate pleasure, and because each of them is pleasant, or because later on they lead to diseases and poverty and many other things like that? Or even if

5 they lead to none of these later, but merely cause pleasure, would they still be bad, just because they cause pleasure in one way or another?" Do you suppose, Protagoras, that they would give any other answer than that they are

e bad not because they produce immediate pleasure, but because of what comes later, diseases and the like?'

'For my part,' said Protagoras, 'I think that that is what most people would say.'

' "And surely in causing diseases they cause pains, and in causing poverty they cause pains." They would agree, I think.'

5 Protagoras agreed.

' "Don't you think that, as Protagoras and I maintain,
354a the only reason these things are bad is that they result in pains and deprive one of other pleasures?" They would agree.'

We both agreed on that.

'Suppose, now, we asked the opposite question, "When you also say that some painful things are good, don't you

5 mean such things as athletic training and warfare and medical treatment by cautery and amputation and drugs and starvation diet? It's these that are good, but painful?" Would they say so?'

'Yes.'

b ' "Now do you call them good because at the time they cause the most extreme suffering and anguish, or because later on they produce things like health and good bodily

5 condition and the safety of the city and rule over others and wealth?" They would agree, I think.'

'Yes.'

' "And are these things good for any other reason than

that they result in pleasures and the relief from and avoidance of pains? Or can you point to any result by reference to which you call them good, other than pleasures and pains?" They would say no, I think.'

'I think so too,' said Protagoras.

' "So you pursue pleasure as good, and avoid pain as evil?" '

He agreed.

' "So it's pain which you regard as evil, and pleasure as good, since you even call enjoyment itself bad when it deprives you of greater pleasures than it has in itself, or leads to pains which are greater than its own pleasures. For if you call enjoyment itself bad for any other reason and by reference to any other result, you would be able to tell us what it is. But you can't." '

'I don't think so either,' said Protagoras.

' "And again, surely it's the same about suffering pain itself. Don't you call suffering pain itself good when it gets rid of greater pains than it has in itself, or when it leads to pleasures which are greater than the pains? For if you refer to any other result when you call suffering pain itself good than the one I say, you will be able to tell us. But you can't." '

'You are quite right,' said Protagoras.

' "Well once again," ' I said, ' "if you asked me, 'But why are you going on at such length and elaboration about this?' I should say, 'I beg your pardon. First of all, it isn't easy to show the real nature of what you call being weaker than pleasures; secondly the whole argument depends on this. But even now you are at liberty to withdraw, if you can give any other account of the good than pleasure, or of evil than pain. Or are you content to say that it is a pleasant life without pains? Now if you are content with that, and aren't able to call anything good or bad except what results in that, listen to what follows. I maintain that, if that is your position, it is absurd for you to say that a man often does bad things though he knows they are bad and could refrain from doing them, because he is driven and overwhelmed by pleasures. And then again

c

5

d

5

e

*
5

355a

5

b

you say that though a man knows what is good, he is not willing to do it, because he is overcome by immediate pleasures. Now that this is absurd will become perfectly clear if we stop using many terms all at once, "pleasant", "painful", "good", and "bad", and instead, since there turned out to be just two things, we use just two names for them, first of all "good" and "bad", and then "pleasant" and "painful". Let's agree on that, then, and say, "Though a man knows that some things are bad, he does them all the same." Now if someone asks "Why?" we shall say "Because he is overcome". "Overcome by what?" he will ask. And we can no longer say "By pleasure", for it has got another name, "good", instead of "pleasure", and so when he says "Overcome by what?" we shall answer, if you please, "Overcome by the good". Now if our questioner happens to be an ill-mannered fellow, he'll burst out laughing and say "What an absurd thing to say! That somebody should do bad things, though he knows they are bad, and doesn't have to do them, because he is overcome by good things. Well," he'll say, "are the good things in your view worth the bad, or not?" Obviously we shall answer, "Not worth the bad. Otherwise the man whom we describe as weaker than pleasures would not have acted wrongly". "What is it then", he will perhaps ask, "which makes good things not worth bad things or bad not worth good? Is it anything apart from the one's being larger and the other smaller; or the one's being more and the other fewer?" We shan't be able to suggest anything else. "It's clear, then," he will say, "that what you mean by being overcome is taking fewer good things at the cost of greater evils." So much for that. Now let's restore the names "pleasant" and "painful" for these very same things, and say "A man does—before we said bad things, but now let's say painful things, in the knowledge that they are painful, because he is overcome by pleasant things, which are, of course, not worth it." And what other way is there for pleasure not to be worth pain, except that one should be more and the other less? And that is a matter of being larger and smaller, or more and fewer, or more and less intense. For if someone said, "But, Socrates, there is a great difference between immediate pleasure and pleasure and pain at a later time," I should say, "Surely not in any other respect than simply pleasure and pain; there isn't any other way they could differ. Rather, like someone who is good at weighing things, add up all the pleasant things and all the painful, and put the element of nearness and distance in the scale as well, and then say which are the more. For if you weigh pleasant things against pleasant, you always have to take the larger and the more, and if you weigh painful against painful, you always have to take the less and the smaller. And if you weigh pleasant against painful, if the painful are outweighed by the pleasant, no matter which are nearer and which more distant, you have to do whatever brings the pleasant about, and if the pleasant are outweighed by the painful, you have to avoid doing it. Isn't that the way it is?" ' I should say." I'm sure that they would not be able to disagree.'

He himself agreed.

' "Now since that is so," I shall say, "answer me this. Do the same magnitudes look bigger when you see them from near at hand, and smaller at a distance, or not?" They will say that they do. "And similarly with thicknesses and numbers? And the same sounds are louder near at hand and softer at a distance?" "Yes." "So if our well-being had depended on taking steps to get large quantities, and avoid small ones, what should we have judged to be the thing that saves our lives? The art of measurement or the power of appearances? The latter, as we saw, confuses us and makes us often change our minds about the same things and vacillate back and forth in our actions and choices of large and small things; but measurement would have made these appearances powerless, and given us peace of mind by showing us the truth and letting us get a firm grasp of it, and would have saved our lives." In the face of this would they agree that it is the art of measurement that would save us, or some other?'

'Measurement,' he agreed.

' "And what if the preservation of our life had depended on a correct choice of odd and even, whenever one had to make a correct choice of a larger number or a smaller, either each kind against itself or one against the other, whether near at hand or at a distance? What would have 357a preserved our life? Knowledge, surely. And surely some sort of measurement, since that is the art concerned with larger and smaller quantities. And since we are concerned with odd and even, it would surely have been none other than arithmetic." Would our friends agree, or not?'

5   Protagoras, too, thought that they would agree.

' "Well then, gentlemen; since we have seen that the preservation of our life depends on a correct choice of pleasure and pain, be it more or less, larger or smaller or

b further or nearer, doesn't it seem that the thing that saves our lives is some technique of measurement, to determine which are more, or less, or equal to one another?" "Yes, certainly." "And since it's measurement, then necessarily

5 it's an art which embodies exact knowledge." "Yes." "Now *which* art, and *what* knowledge, we shall inquire later. But this suffices to show *that* it is knowledge, and to provide the demonstration that Protagoras and I are re-

c quired to give in reply to your question. You raised it, if you remember, when we were in agreement that nothing is more powerful than knowledge, and that no matter where it is it always conquers pleasure and everything

5 else. You then said that pleasure often conquers even the man who is in possession of knowledge, and when we didn't agree, it was then that you asked us, 'Well, if this experience isn't being overcome by pleasure, what is it

d then? What do you call it? Tell us.' If we had then straight away said 'Error' you would have laughed at us; but now, if you laugh at us you will be laughing at yourselves. For you have agreed that those who go wrong in their choice

5 of pleasures and pains—which is to say, of good and bad things—go wrong from lack of knowledge, and not merely of knowledge, but, as you have already further conceded, of measurement. And you surely know yourselves that

e wrong action done without knowledge is done in error. So

this is what being weaker than pleasure is, the greatest of all errors, for which Protagoras here and Hippias and Prodicus claim to have the cure. But because you think that it is something other than error you neither consult these sophists yourselves nor send your sons to them to have them taught this; you don't believe that it can be taught, so you hang on to your money instead of giving it to them, and as a result you do badly both as private individuals and in public affairs."

358a1–360e5 Socrates applies the conclusion of the fore-going discussion to the disputed case of courage and cow-ardice, obliging Protagoras to assent to his thesis that the coward too goes wrong through error. Hence Protagoras is obliged to withdraw his contention that it is possible to be courageous while lacking in knowledge.

That's what we should have said in reply to the majority. And now, on behalf of Protagoras and myself, I ask you, Hippias and Prodicus (for you can answer jointly), whether you think that what I am saying is true or false.'

They were all completely satisfied that it was true.

'You agree, then,' I said, 'that what is pleasant is good, and what is painful bad. I leave aside our friend Prodicus' distinction of names; for whether you call it "pleasant" or "delightful" or "enjoyable", or however you care to apply such names, my dear Prodicus, give your answer according to the sense of my question.'

Prodicus laughed, and indicated his agreement, and so did the rest.

'Well, gentlemen,' I said, 'what about this? Aren't all actions praiseworthy which lead to a painless and pleasant life? And isn't praiseworthy activity good and beneficial?'

They agreed.

'So if what is pleasant is good,' I said, 'no one who either knows or believes that something else is better than what he is doing, and is in his power to do, subsequently does the other, when he can do what is better. Nor is giving in to oneself anything other than error, nor controlling oneself anything other than wisdom.'

They all agreed.

'Well now. Is this what you mean by error, having false opinions and being mistaken about matters of importance?'

They all agreed to that as well.

'Now surely,' I said, 'no one freely goes for bad things or things he believes to be bad; it's not, it seems to me, in human nature to be prepared to go for what you think to be bad in preference to what is good. And when you are forced to choose one of two evils, nobody will choose the greater when he can have the lesser. Isn't that so?'

All of us agreed to all of that.

'Well, then,' I said, 'is there something that you call fear and apprehension? And is it the same thing as I mean? (This is a question for you, Prodicus.) I mean by this an expectation of evil, whether you call it fear or apprehension.'

Protagoras and Hippias thought that that's what fear and apprehension are, while Prodicus thought it was apprehension, but not fear.

'Well, it doesn't make any difference, Prodicus,' I said. 'The point is this. If what has just been said is true, will any man be willing to go for what he fears, when he can go for what he doesn't fear? Or is that impossible, according to what we have agreed? For if anyone fears something, it was agreed that he thinks it bad; and no one who thinks anything bad goes for it or takes it of his own free will.'

That too was agreed by everyone.

'On that basis, then, Prodicus and Hippias,' I said, 'let Protagoras defend the correctness of his first answer to me. I don't mean what he said right at the beginning; for at that point he said that while there are five parts of excellence none is like any other, but each has its own separate power. I don't mean that, but what he said later. For later he said that four of the five resemble one another fairly closely, but one is altogether different from the others, namely courage. His evidence was the following:

"You will find, Socrates, men who are totally irreligious, unjust, wanton, and ignorant, but very courageous; that's how you will know that courage is very different from the other parts of excellence." I was very surprised at his answer at the time, and even more now that I have gone into the question together with you. So I asked him if he called courageous men daring. "Yes, and ready," he said.   c
Do you recall that answer, Protagoras?' I said.

'I do.'

'Well, now,' I said, 'tell us, what are courageous men ready for? The same things as cowards?'

'No.'

'Different things, then.'

'Yes,' he said.

'Do cowards go for things which they are confident   5
about, and courageous men for fearful things?'

'So it's generally said, Socrates.'

'True,' I said, 'but that isn't what I'm asking. What do   d
you say the courageous are ready for? Fearful things, in the belief that they are fearful, or not?'

'But it's just been shown by what you've said,' he replied, 'that that's impossible.'

'That's true as well,' I said. 'So if that demonstration   5
was correct, no one goes for things that he regards as fearful, since giving in to oneself turned out to be error.'

He agreed.

'But now everyone, coward and courageous alike, goes for what he is confident about, and in this way, at any   e
rate, cowards and courageous go for the same things.'

'But, Socrates,' he said, 'the things that cowards go for are exactly the opposite of those that the courageous go for. For instance, courageous men are willing to go to war, but cowards aren't.'

'Is it praiseworthy to go,' I said, 'or disgraceful?'   5

'Praiseworthy.'

'So if it's praiseworthy, we agreed previously that it is good; for we agreed that all praiseworthy actions are good.'

'That's true; I remain of that opinion.'

'You are right,' I said. 'But which of them is it you say 360a are not willing to go to war, though that is something praiseworthy and good?'

'Cowards,' he said.

'Well, now,' I said, 'if it's praiseworthy and good, is it also pleasant?'

'Well, that's what was agreed,' he said.

'So cowards are unwilling, in full knowledge of the facts, to go for what is more praiseworthy and better and pleasanter?'

'But if we agree to that,' he said, 'we shall contradict our previously agreed conclusions.'

'And what about the courageous man? Does he not go for what is more praiseworthy and better and pleasanter?'

'I have to agree,' he said.

'Now in general, when a courageous man is afraid, his fear is not something disgraceful, nor his confidence when he is confident?'

'That's right,' he said.

'And if not disgraceful, are they not praiseworthy?'

He agreed.

'And if praiseworthy, good as well?'

'Yes.'

'Now by contrast the fear and the confidence of cowards, madmen, and the foolhardy are disgraceful?'

He agreed.

'And is their confidence disgraceful and bad for any other reason than ignorance and error?'

'It's as you say,' he said.

'Well, now, do you call what makes a man a coward, cowardice or courage?'

'I call it cowardice,' he said.

'And didn't it turn out that they are cowards as a result of their error about what is to be feared?'

'Certainly,' he said.

'So it's in consequence of that error that they are cowards?'

He agreed.

'And you agree that what makes them cowards is cowardice?'

64

He assented.

'So cowardice proves to be error about what is to be feared and what isn't?'

He nodded.

'But now,' I said, 'the opposite of cowardice is courage.'   d

'Yes.'

'Now wisdom about what is to be feared and what isn't is the opposite of error about that.'

At that he nodded once again.

'And error about that is cowardice?'

With great reluctance he nodded at that.

'So wisdom about what is to be feared and what isn't   5
is courage, since it is the opposite of error about that?'

At this he wasn't even willing to nod agreement, but remained silent. And I said, 'What's this, Protagoras? Won't you even answer yes or no?'

'Carry on yourself,' he said.

'I've only one more question to ask you,' I said. 'Do   e
you still think, as you did at the beginning, that some men are altogether ignorant, but very courageous?'

'I see that you insist, Socrates,' he said, 'that I must answer. So I'll oblige you; I declare that from what we   5
have agreed it seems to me impossible.'

360e6–361d6 *Socrates summarizes the course of the argument.*

'Indeed I've no other object', I said, 'in asking all these questions than to try to find out the truth about excellence, and especially what it is itself. For I know that once 361a
that were apparent we should become perfectly clear on the question about which each of us has had so much to say, I maintaining that excellence can't be taught, and you that it can. And it seems to me that the conclusion we have just reached is jeering at us like an accuser. And if   5
it could speak, it would say "How absurd you are, both of you. You, Socrates, began by saying that excellence   b
can't be taught, and now you are insisting on the opposite, trying to show that all things are knowledge, justice,

soundness of mind, even courage, from which it would follow that excellence most certainly could be taught. For if excellence were anything other than knowledge, as Pro-

5   tagoras was trying to make out, it would obviously not be teachable. But now, if it turns out to consist wholly in knowledge, as you insist, Socrates, it will be astonishing if it can't be taught. Protagoras, on the other hand, first assumed that it can be taught, but now seems to be taking

c   the opposite view and insisting that it turns out to be practically anything rather than knowledge; and so it most certainly couldn't be taught." For my part, Protagoras, when I see all this in such terrible confusion, I am desper-

5   ately anxious to have it all cleared up, and I should like to follow up our discussion by considering the nature of excellence, and then returning to the question of whether or not it can be taught. I shouldn't like that Epimetheus

d   (Afterthought) of yours to fool us with his tricks in our discussion, the way he neglected us in distributing his gifts, as you said. I preferred Prometheus (Forethought) to

5   Epimetheus in the story; it's because I have forethought for my life as a whole that I go into all these questions. And as I said at the beginning, if you were willing I should be most happy to examine them with you.'

361d7–362a4   *The farewells.*

'For my part, Socrates,' said Protagoras, 'I applaud your enthusiasm and the way you pursue your arguments. I

e   don't think I'm an inferior person in any respect, but in particular I'm the last man to bear a grudge; for I've said to many people that of all those I've met I like you far the best, especially of those of your age. And I declare that I should not be surprised if you became famous for your

5   wisdom. As to these questions, we shall pursue them some other time, whenever you wish; but now it's time to turn to something else.'

362a   'Indeed that's what we should do,' I said, 'if you prefer. In fact, quite a while ago it was time for me to go where I said, but I stayed to oblige our friend Callias.'

That was the end of the conversation, and we left.

BIOGRAPHICAL NOTES ON
THE MAIN CHARACTERS OF
THE *PROTAGORAS*

Socrates 470/69–399 BC. Born in Athens, where he spent all his life, apart from periods of military service, engaged in the informal discussion of philosophical (mainly ethical) topics. Though he never engaged in formal teaching, he gathered round himself a circle of mainly younger men, including Plato, many of whom were opposed to the extreme form of democracy current in Athens. He was put to death on vague charges of impiety and corruption of youth, which were probably politically inspired. His philosophical views and methods were a major influence on Plato, but the ascription of any specific doctrine to Socrates is a matter of much controversy. He wrote nothing himself, but in the fourth century many accounts of his personality and teaching were written, mostly friendly, but some hostile, with different degrees of approximation to historical truth. The most substantial element of this literature to survive is the dialogues of Plato; Socrates also figures in a number of works by Xenophon. The *Clouds* of Aristophanes, first produced in 423, gives a contemporary caricature.

Protagoras c.490–420. From Abdera, on the north coast of the Aegean. The first professional sophist, i.e. itinerant professor of higher education. He had a long and successful career, travelling widely throughout the Greek world and making very large sums of money. He aimed to teach upper-class youths how to attain personal and political success, putting considerable emphasis on skill in speech and argument, in which he developed a systematic method of teaching. He is said to have written a number of works in this area, and on more general ethical and philosophical topics. A few quotations are preserved, expressing agnosticism on the existence of the gods and extreme subjectivism, according to which every belief is true for the person who holds it. The latter position is criticized at length by Plato in the *Theaetetus*.

Hippias from Elis in the north-west Peloponnese. His dates are uncertain, but Plato makes him describe himself in the *Greater Hippias* (282e) as considerably younger than Protagoras, while *Apol.* 19e indicates that he was still alive in 399. He too made a considerable reputation and fortune, and frequently represented his city on diplomatic missions. He was a polymath, who wrote on and taught subjects including mathematics, science, history, rhetoric, literature, ethics, and a range of practical crafts. Nothing of his work survives. He appears in two Platonic dialogues, both entitled *Hippias*; the authenticity of one, the *Greater* (i.e. *Longer*) *Hippias*, is questioned by some scholars.

Prodicus from Ceos, an island off the southern tip of Attica. Dates uncertain, but still alive in 399 (*Apol.* 19e). Like Hippias, he used the opportunities provided by diplomatic missions to build up an international clientele. He was primarily a teacher of rhetoric, whose speciality was the distinction of near-synonyms; many examples are given in the *Protagoras* and elsewhere. In a number of places Plato makes Socrates say, sometimes apparently ironically, sometimes not, that he is indebted to this technique. Prodicus' other interests included ethics, theology, and science. All that survives of his work is a paraphrase by Xenophon (*Mem.* 2. 1. 21–34) of his fable of the choice of Heracles between Virtue and Pleasure.

Alcibiades c.450–404. Athenian. He rose to political prominence at an early age, and was one of the leaders of the policy of ambitious imperialism which led to the disastrous Sicilian expedition of 415, of which he was appointed one of the commanders. Implicated in an act of sacrilege committed shortly before the expedition sailed, he fled to Sparta to escape trial, and took an active part in the war against Athens. Subsequently reinstated at Athens he gained some military successes, but, once more attracting popular suspicion, went into exile a second time and was murdered with the connivance of the Athenian government. On his relations with Socrates see Explanatory Note on 309a2. The Platonic corpus contains two dialogues entitled *Alcibiades*, of doubtful authenticity. He plays a prominent part in the *Symposium*.

Callias c.455–c.370. Member of a distinguished Athenian family, he was chiefly known for his lavish expenditure, including large sums spent on sophists, which dissipated the family fortune. His sister married Alcibiades subsequently to the dramatic date of the *Protagoras*.

Critias c.460–403. Athenian, first cousin of Plato's mother. An associate of Alcibiades, he was opposed to the Athenian democracy, and was one of the most extreme among the Thirty Tyrants, the oppressive dictatorship which seized power in Athens from 404 to 403. He was killed in the fighting which accompanied the overthrow of the tyranny. He was a poet, dramatist, and prose writer, of whose works some fragments survive (DK 88). He has a prominent part in the *Charmides*.

For information on others appearing or mentioned in the dialogue, see Explanatory Notes.

EXPLANATORY NOTES

THE dramatic date of the dialogue is shortly before the outbreak of the First Peloponnesian War, probably about 433; Socrates is about 37, Alcibiades about 17.

309a *Alcibiades*: it is clear that the charge of 'corrupting the young men', which was one of the accusations on which Socrates was put to death (Xen. *Mem.* 1. 1. 1, D.L. 2. 40), was based at least partly on his supposed responsibility for the subsequent political careers of some of his young associates, notably Alcibiades and Critias (see Biographical Notes). Plato makes Socrates allude to this in the *Apology* (33a–b) without mentioning names, since a recent amnesty had made it impossible for his accusers to bring a direct charge. Xenophon, writing some years later, refers directly (*Mem.* 1. 2. 12–16) to the accusation (probably made explicitly by the fourth-century pamphleteer Polycrates, who wrote an *Accusation of Socrates* containing charges which could not be made openly at the trial) that 'Critias and Alcibiades, after having been associates of Socrates, inflicted a great number of evils on the state'. *Rep.* 6. 494b–495b contains a clear allusion to the career of Alcibiades and his relations with Socrates. Cf. Guthrie iii. 345, 378–83.

Socrates is regularly represented by Plato as being physically and emotionally attracted to young men of fine appearance and intelligence. The most striking and explicit description of his feelings is given (in the first person) at *Charmides* 155c–e, but other references abound, e.g. *Symp.* 216d, *Alc. I* 103a–104d, *Gorg.* 481d. There is no reason to doubt Plato's explicit statements, nor his equally explicit testimony that Socrates gave his feelings no physical expression, but rather sought to promote the moral and intellectual development of the young men who attracted him; cf. especially Alcibiades' account of his relations with Socrates at *Symp.* 215a–219d. This is consistent with the theory of love which Socrates puts into the mouth of the wise woman Diotima at *Symp.* 201d–212a.

For further discussions of Socrates' attitude to sex and love see Guthrie iii. 390–8; Dover, *Greek Homosexuality*, 153–70.

310a Hippocrates is probably a historical person, as are most of the characters in Plato's dialogues, but nothing is known about him beyond what is said in this dialogue.

311b *Hippocrates of Cos*: a contemporary of Socrates and the founder of the most influential school of Greek medicine.

311c Polycleitus and Pheidias were the two most celebrated sculptors of the fifth century.

311e *a sophist*: the Greek *sophistēs* lacks the specific pejorative implication (of dishonesty in argument) which attaches to its English derivative. From its original use as equivalent to *sophos* 'expert' or, more specifically 'sage', it had by this period acquired the technical sense 'itinerant purveyor of higher education'. See Guthrie iii. 27–36, with refs. p. 27 n. 1, and Kerferd, *SM* ch. 4.

312a Hippocrates' embarrassment at the thought of becoming a sophist himself reflects the ambivalent attitude of contemporary opinion towards the profession. On the one hand they became extremely wealthy and were received in the houses of the great. On the other, they were gravely suspect to conservative opinion as a potential source of corruption for the young (*Prot.* 316c–d, *Meno* 91c, Arist. *Clouds passim*, see Dover's introduction, xxxii–lxiv).

312b The reading-master not only taught reading and writing, but also gave instruction in the works of the poets, laying much emphasis on their ethical content (cf. 325c–326a). This, together with music and physical training, was the staple of elementary education, the only formal education available until the advent of the sophists. For Plato's view of its inadequacies, see especially *Rep.* 2. 376e–3. 412b.

312b In view of its theological connotations, 'soul' has a narrower sense than the Greek *psuchē*, which signifies the self in its non-bodily aspects, embracing intellect, will, desires, and emotions. Here the most natural translation would be 'entrust yourself', but since at 313a we have the specific contrast between bodily and non-bodily aspects of the self, for which 'body' and 'soul' are the best pair of contrasting English terms, 'soul' is used for *psuchē* here too.

312c *as the name implies*: Hippocrates derives the noun *sophistēs* (wrongly) from *sophos* = 'wise, learned' + the root of the verb 'to know', *epistasthai*. It is in fact derived, via the regular 'agent' termination, from the verb *sophizesthai*, 'to be wise'.

312d–e Socrates relies on a single example, that of the music teacher, to establish the implied general proposition that, whenever A makes B an effective speaker, he does so by imparting to *B* some specialized knowledge which is to be the subject-matter of *B*'s speeches. The establishment of a general conclusion on the basis of two or three key instances is a characteristic feature of Socrates' argumentation in Plato's dialogues, occurring many times in this dialogue (e.g. 332c, 349e–350a) and elsewhere; Aristotle indicates (*Met.* M4, 1978^{b}27–9) that this kind of argument was characteristic of the historical Socrates.

314e–315a Callias' mother was formerly married to the famous statesman Pericles, by whom she had the two sons named here. Both, like their father, died in the great epidemic which struck Athens shortly after the beginning of the Peloponnesian War. On the dissolution of that marriage she married Callias' father Hipponicus.

315a *Charmides*: Plato's maternal uncle. He was associated with his cousin Critias in the oligarchic revolution of 404, and was killed in the fighting when it was overthrown. He is the principal character in the dialogue which bears his name.

315a *Philippides*: member of a distinguished Athenian family.

Antimoerus seems not to have fulfilled the promise suggested, as he is known only from this passage. Mende, like Abdera, was a subject city of the Athenian empire on the N. Aegean coast.

315b *procession*: lit. 'chorus'. The elaborate manœuvres of Protagoras' entourage are compared to the formation dancing of the chorus in a tragedy or comedy.

Plato is perhaps recalling portrayals of gatherings of sophists in comedy, such as Eupolis' *Flatterers* (produced 421), which was set in the house of Callias and included Protagoras and Alcibiades among its characters, or Ameipsias' *Konnos* (produced 423, the same year as Aristophanes' *Clouds*), which had a chorus of 'Thinkers' and Socrates as a character.

315b Here and at 315c Socrates speaks with the words of Odysseus, describing his visit to the underworld, where he sees the ghosts (Greek *skiai*, lit. 'shadows') of the dead. A similar allusion occurs at *Meno* 100a, where Socrates says that an outstanding citizen (*politikos*) who was capable of making others outstanding would be like Tiresias, whom Homer describes (*Od.* 10. 494–5) as 'the only one alive of those in Hades, while they flit about as shadows'. The resemblance is not coincidental. At *Gorg.* 521d Socrates claims to be the only genuine *politikos*, since he alone cares for the real (i.e. the moral) good of his fellow citizens. Shadows are a mere image or semblance of reality (*Rep.* 509e, *Soph.* 265b–c), and the sophist is a maker of misleading images, in particular of counterfeits of genuine instances of knowledge (*Soph.* 232–6, 264–8). The representation of the sophists as ghosts indicates immediately that they are mere shadows compared to Socrates, who is 'the real thing as regards excellence' (*Meno* 100a), and derivatively that their purported expertise is mere semblance.

315c   *Eryximachus*: a doctor. He appears with his friend Phaedrus in the *Symposium*, where he discusses love in terms of medical theory. He was implicated in the sacrilege of 415 (see Biographical Note on Alcibiades).

315c   *Phaedrus*: appears in the *Phaedrus* and *Symposium* as an amateur of oratory, with a particular interest in the theme of love. He too was exiled as having been implicated in the events of 415. Myrrinus was a district of Athens (cf. 'Cerameis' d7).

    Andron: mentioned at *Gorg.* 487c as a friend of Callicles. He was a member of the oligarchic government of the Four Hundred, who held power briefly in 411.

315d   *Pausanias*: appears in the *Symposium*. His relationship with Agathon is mentioned by Xenophon (*Symp.* 8. 32). Nothing else is known about him.

315e   *Agathon*: at this time a boy of about 15, he became a prominent tragedian. The dinner-party in the *Symposium* is held at his house to celebrate his first victory in the dramatic competitions in 416. Some fragments of his plays survive. Aristophanes makes fun of him in *The Thesmophoriazusae*, produced in 411.

315e   *Adeimantus . . . son of Cepis*: otherwise unknown.

    Adeimantus . . . son of Leucolophides: another prominent Athenian implicated in the sacrilege of 415. He was subsequently a commander (sometimes together with Alcibiades) in the later campaigns of the war, and was accused of treachery after the final defeat of Athens in 404.

316d   *Iccus*: a noted athlete and trainer, from Taras in south Italy (mod. Taranto).

316e   *Herodicus*: a doctor and trainer, from Selymbria, a Megarian colony near Byzantium.

316e   *Agathocles . . . Pythocleides*: prominent musicians and music teachers.

317b–c On Protagoras' long career and good reputation cf. *Meno* 91e, from which we learn that his career spanned forty years and that his good reputation lasted up to and well beyond his death. This is convincing proof of the falsity of the later tradition (DK 80 A 1–4 and 12) according to which he was forced to flee from Athens on a charge of impiety and was lost at sea in doing so.

317c This, together with the *Meno* passage just mentioned, which tells us that Protagoras died about the age of 70, is the best evidence for his dates. He must have been twenty to thirty years older than Socrates, hence born some time between 500 and 490, and must therefore have died some time between 430 and 420. Since he is referred to as still alive in a comedy by Eupolis, *The Flatterers*, produced in 422/1 (DK 80 A 1 and 11), his dates must be approximately 490–420. He had therefore been practising as a sophist for close on thirty years and possibly more by the time of the dramatic date of the *Protagoras*.

318b Zeuxis or Zeuxippus, from Heraclea in the Gulf of Taranto, was one of the best-known painters of the period.

318c Orthagoras was a celebrated virtuoso of the *aulos*, a reed instrument resembling the modern oboe or clarinet.

319a *to make men into good citizens*: the Greek might also be rendered as 'to make citizens into good men', or 'to turn out good citizens'.

We find it startling that Socrates should equate teaching the art of how to run a city with making men into good citizens, and that Protagoras should accept this equation. Modern thought makes a clear distinction between the good politician and the good statesman on the one hand, who excel in the performance of (different) specific tasks, and the good citizen on the other. This distinction was less clear-cut in an extreme democracy such as fifth-century Athens, where every adult male citizen was a member of the supreme deliberative assembly and might find himself obliged by lot to perform a variety of executive functions. See next note.

319e *excellence*: used here and generally (see end of this note) to render the Greek *aretē*. This word functions as the abstract noun from the adjective 'good'; anything which is a good x, or (generally equivalently) which does well the activity which is characteristic of x's *ipso facto* possesses the *aretē* of or appropriate to x's. Human *aretē* falls within this general schema; a man may achieve excellence in some specific role, e.g. as a boxer, or he may possess qualities in virtue of which he is a good or admirable *man*. In the former case his *aretē* is that of a boxer, in the latter it is human *aretē*. The conventional rendering 'virtue', with its specifically moral connotations, is highly misleading; while fifth-century Greeks did indeed count some moral virtues as prominent among the qualities that make a man a good man, they recognized much else besides. The excellence which is immediately in question is that of a citizen, of which the paradigm example is a statesman such as Pericles, who was successful both in attaining personal power and reputation and in enlarging the power and reputation of the city. The question of whether excellence can be taught, as originally introduced by Socrates in this passage, is the question whether it is possible to teach someone how to attain that sort of success. As remarked above (Introduction, p. xvi), Protagoras shifts the discussion to the question of whether it is possible to teach someone to be a good citizen in the sense of a fair-minded and law-abiding citizen. No distinction is drawn between being a good citizen in that sense and being a good man.

320a *Cleinias*: at *Alc. I* 118e Alcibiades bluntly describes his younger brother as a madman. Nothing is known of him apart from these two passages.

320a *Ariphron*: brother of Pericles, with whom he was joint guardian of Alcibiades and Cleinias (Plut. *Alc.* 1. 1).

320c ff. The Greeks were familiar with two opposed accounts of human development: (*a*) that represented here, the naturalistic tradition, developed in the fifth century from traditional antecedents, of progress from primitive beginnings; (*b*) the older Hesiodic tradition of progressive decline from an original state of innocence. Plato's own theory (*Pol.* 273–4, *Tim.* 72–3, *Crit.* 110–12, *Laws* 3. 676–82) combines elements of both traditions.

There has been much discussion of the question whether Protagoras' defence is based on an actual work of his (see Guthrie iii. 64 n. 1). In view of the considerable interest in the fifth century in the origins of civilization (see Guthrie iii. 60–84 and Kahn in Kerferd (ed.)), and in view of the fact that the list of titles of works attributed to Protagoras includes one 'On the original state of things' (D.L. 9. 55), it is perfectly plausible that it is. On the other hand, nothing in the dialogue indicates that Protagoras' story might be familiar to his audience. In reply to Socrates' first objection, namely that the Athenians think that there are no experts on how to run the city, Protagoras argues that, on the contrary, they and everyone else regard all citizens as experts in that field. He supports this by giving, in the story, an account of the nature of political expertise via a speculative account of how it may be supposed to have developed in man. The essential feature of this reconstruction is that people, living naturally in small scattered groups, probably corresponding to families, are driven by necessity to form larger communities, but find that hostility between different groups makes communal life impossible. What is lacking is a sense of social solidarity transcending the natural kinship group, which would enable every individual to see every other as possessing rights not in virtue of a natural bond of kinship, but merely as a member of the community, and which would in consequence generate habits of self-restraint and respect for others. That is to say, they lacked *dikē* and *aidōs* (or their prosaic equivalents *dikaiosunē* and *sōphrosunē*). Moreover, these dispositions must not be the preserve of a special élite, but must be shared by all, for anyone lacking in them is potentially disruptive of the community. Gradually, the story tells us, by a long process of trial and error, this universal habit of mind was built up, finally allowing organized communities to develop.

Protagoras nowhere explains why one has to have special expertise to be entitled to speak on technical matters, but nothing beyond mere adulthood and rationality to speak on matters of public policy. He probably assumes that, while a technical expert is one who knows how best to attain an agreed end, questions of policy are themselves largely questions about what ends are to be pursued, and further that these questions are not susceptible of right and wrong answers, and hence there can be no one who is especially qualified to answer them. Rather, each individual has to make up his mind how he or she wants to live and what sort of community he or she wants to live in.

That doctrine would follow naturally from the more general subjectivist thesis which Protagoras maintained. Since he held that in general what each person believes is true for him or her, which I take to imply that the notion of impersonal truth, according to which a belief is true or false *simpliciter*, is an empty one, it will follow that what each person believes on matters of public policy is true for him or her, and that no view can be said to be just true or false. Since no opinion on how to conduct affairs is truer than any other, no one can claim any special authority for his or her opinion. But the *polis* must act in some way or other. Hence the most sensible rule is to let all opinions be heard and to act on the one which wins the most general assent. Hence Protagorean subjectivism might quite naturally (though not, of course, necessarily) lead to support for democracy.

321e Athena was associated with spinning and weaving, with pottery, and with the cultivation of the olive. The reference may be to any of these crafts.

322a *get food from the earth*: the reference is certainly to hunting and gathering, and perhaps also to agriculture.

323a Protagoras' position here (repeated at 324d–325a and at 326e–327a) is prima facie inconsistent with his commonsense admission (329e, 349d) that not every member of a civilized community is a good man. He would presumably reply that men who are unjust etc. by conventional standards are none the less good in the minimal sense required for participation in social life (327c–e). But while that defence removes the inconsistency, it prevents Protagoras from meeting Socrates' objection to his claim to teach excellence in the accepted sense.

323c Protagoras has so far attempted to show (*a*) what political expertise consists in and (*b*) that it is universally believed that everyone possesses it. He now attempts to show that there is also a universal belief that it is not a natural endowment, but a skill acquired through teaching.

323c–324d Modern discussions of punishment distinguish three main areas of dispute:
  (i) The definitional question
      What is the definition of the concept of punishment?
  (ii) Questions of justification
      (*a*) What is the aim of the practice of punishment?
      (*b*) Does that aim show the practice to be rationally or morally justified?
  (iii) Questions of distribution
      (*a*) What class of person is in general liable for punishment?
      (*b*) What amounts of punishment are appropriate either in general or in particular cases?

Protagoras says nothing about (i). He is best understood as giving, in undifferentiated form, answers to qq. (ii) and (iii) as follows:

- (ii) (a) The aim of the practice of punishment is the discouragement of socially undesirable behaviour.
  - (b) That aim shows the practice to be justified.
- (iii) (a) (?All and) only those offenders should be punished whose punishment may be expected to prevent further wrongful acts on the part either of those punished or of others.
  - (b) The appropriate amount of punishment is in every case that which may be expected to be most effective in preventing further wrongdoing.

324d Protagoras now turns ostensibly to the second of Socrates' objections. It is not in fact directly answered till 326e6, since the answer requires a prior account of how the sons of good men are taught.

327d *Pherecrates*: a writer of comedies, of which only a few quotations survive. His play *The Savages* was produced at the Lenaea (the earlier of the two great annual dramatic festivals at Athens, held in January) in 420. As the weight of evidence for the dramatic date points to about 433, it is best to treat this as an anachronism, of which there are other instances in Plato.

327d Eurybatus and Phrynondas were apparently real persons, whose names became proverbial for wickedness.

328c–d Summary of conclusions reached. Protagoras claims to have established (a) that one can be taught to be a good citizen, (b) that the Athenians believe that one can, and (c) that it is not surprising that the sons of good men sometimes turn out badly and vice versa.

329c–d Socrates asks Protagoras whether the names of the specific excellences, justice, holiness, etc. pick out different features of the individual, as e.g. 'sight' and 'hearing' name different senses, or whether all those names are names of the same thing. Protagoras' reply makes it clear that his position is the former. The development of the rest of the dialogue shows that Socrates holds the latter position, but there has been much scholarly dispute on exactly how that position should be understood. See Introduction.

329d–331b Socrates' argument depends on an equivocation between two senses of 'like', (i) having any characteristic in common, and (ii) having every characteristic in common. While Protagoras maintains that the excellences are not like each other in sense (ii), Socrates relies on sense (i) to derive his conclusion that, if one excellence has any quality (e.g. if holiness is holy) any other excellence must lack that quality. Protagoras' reply at 331d–e comes near to identifying this flaw in the argument, indicating that Plato was probably conscious that the argument was unsound. On the implications for our view of Plato's intentions in writing the dialogue, see Introduction.

330c The ascription of an attribute to itself (self-predication) is facilitated by the fact that in Greek attributes are regularly designated by the adjective preceded by the definite article, e.g. 'the beautiful' (= 'beauty'), 'the just' (= 'justice'). Hence 'The just is just' (i.e. the attribute justice *possesses* the attribute justice) is liable to be confused with 'The just is the just' (i.e. the attribute justice *is* the attribute justice). Attributes are thought of in an undifferentiated way as 'things' (cf. c1), which are manifested in or by other things, but whose primary manifestation is in their own being. Hence it is natural for Plato to say (d–e) that unless holiness were itself holy, nothing else would be; if holiness were not manifested in its own being there would not be any such thing to be manifested in other things. In developing this line of thought Plato is led to the position (*Ph.* 74a–d, *Symp.* 211a–b, *Rep.* 5. 476a–480a) that at least some important classes of attributes are completely manifested *only* by themselves, in contrast with their more or less imperfect or incomplete manifestation by observable instances, a position central to his theory of Forms. See Frede, introduction to Lombardo and Bell's translation, xxiv–xxvi.

332a–334a For discussion of these arguments see Taylor, *Protagoras* comm.

332a *act sensibly*: the context requires that the noun *sōphrosunē* and its cognates (including the verb *sōphronein*, which occurs here) be understood in the basic sense of 'soundness of mind, good sense' rather than in the derived sense of 'self-control, mastery of the bodily appetites', which predominates elsewhere in Plato (e.g. *Gorg.* 491d etc., *Rep.* 4. 430e, etc.) and which is taken by Aristotle (*EN* 3. 10) as the central sense. Stage i of the argument for step 2 depends on two premisses 'If anyone acts rightly he *sōphronei*' and 'If anyone acts

79

wrongly he does not *sōphronei*'. While these premises are at least reasonably plausible if *sōphronei* is taken as 'acts sensibly, shows good sense', they seem plainly false if the verb is read as 'shows self-control', since in some cases of right and wrong action the bodily appetites or similar impulses (e.g. anger) are not involved. In addition to this basic use of the term *sōphrosunē*, which is regular from its earliest occurrences in Homer to the fourth century BC and later, the word comes to stand for specific manifestations of soundness of mind, especially proper consciousness of one's own position relative to the claims of others, and hence respect or reverence (whether towards gods or men), self-abnegation, moderation, and modesty, and also mastery of one's desires, especially the bodily desires.

In the *Charmides*, an early dialogue devoted to the subject of *sōphrosunē*, mastery of appetite does not figure among the suggested accounts of the virtue; instead, the accounts offered are decorum, modesty (*aidōs*), performance of one's proper role (cf. the political sense mentioned above), the doing of good things, and self-knowledge, while Socrates hints, without asserting, that the correct account is the knowledge of good and bad (esp. 171d–176a). It seems clear that the main purpose of the *Charmides* is to explore various aspects and possible developments of the traditional conception of *sōphrosunē* as soundness of mind, in which the term is virtually synonymous with one kind of *sophia*. In view of the statement of Xenophon (*Mem.* 3. 9. 4) that 'Socrates made no distinction between *sophia* and *sōphrosunē*, but used to say that the man who could recognize and make use of fine and good things and recognize and avoid shameful things (cf. *Charm.*) was *sophos* and *sōphrōn*', it is possible that the view of *sōphrosunē* which predominates in the *Charmides* and *Protagoras* is closer to Socrates' own than the greater emphasis on self-control as the primary manifestation of soundness of mind which we find in the *Gorgias*, *Republic*, and elsewhere, which may represent a specifically Platonic development.

334a–c The central point here is that 'good for' is a relational expression, like 'taller than', 'half of', 'father of', etc. Hence there is no single answer to the question 'Is *x* good?', any more than there is a single answer to the question 'Is *x* the half?' or 'Is *x* to the right?' In all cases the question must first be completed by specification of that to which the relation is held, and in all cases we must expect the answer that *x* has the relation to one thing but does not have it to something else. This does not imply that if anyone believes that something is good, then that thing is good (for him), i.e. the application to goodness of the general thesis of Protagorean subjectivism. The observation that manure is good for roots but bad for leaves neither entails nor follows from the thesis that whatever anyone believes to be good is good (for the person who believes it).

Protagoras does not here espouse any version of evaluative relativism, i.e. the doctrine that the standards by which things are judged good or bad vary in different circumstances (e.g. in different cultures, at different historical epochs, according to the different interests of different individuals) and that there is no second-order criterion by which it is possible to judge any standard more correct than any other. Protagoras' examples, which are all of facts of nature, e.g. that oil is bad for plants, do indeed presuppose agreed standards of what counts as a good state for plants and animals, but there is no reason to suppose that Plato represents him as looking on these as culture-relative, nor is it clear that they are in fact.

335a This is one of the pieces of evidence which indicate that debating contests conducted according to agreed rules were part of the characteristic activity of sophists. Other relevant passages are 338a–b, where Hippias suggests the appointment of an umpire for the present discussion, and *Hipp. Min.* 363c–364a, where Hippias describes how he goes regularly to the Olympic Games to take part in contests (*agōnizesthai*, the regular word for athletic and similar competition) of question and answer and has never yet been beaten. According to Diogenes Laertius, Protagoras was the first to institute such contests (9. 52).

335e Crison from Himera in Sicily won the sprint at three successive Olympic Games, in 448, 444, and 440.

courier: not an athlete, but a messenger, such as Pheidippides who ran from Athens to summon help from Sparta on the occasion of the campaign of Marathon in 490 (Hdt. 6. 105. 1).

337a–c This is the most important single piece of evidence for the semantic distinctions in which Prodicus specialized. Other instances of distinctions which are said to be in the style of Prodicus occur at 340a (between 'wish' and 'desire'), 340c ('be' and 'become'), 358a ('pleasant', 'delightful', and 'enjoy-able'), 358d ('fear' and 'apprehension'), *Meno* 75e ('end' and 'limit'), *Lach.* 197b–d ('fearless' and 'courageous'), *Charm.* 163b–d ('do' and 'make' or 'work'), and *Euthyd.* 277e–278a ('learn' and 'understand', both represented by the verb *manthanein*). The method exemplified in this section is a mixture of classification of actual usage and prescription for linguistic reform.

337d The distinction between nature and convention to which Hippias refers was of considerable importance in fifth-century thought. There are in fact two contrasts. On the one hand there is what is the case in reality or in the nature of things (*phusei*), i.e. independently of human choice or convention. Opposed to that we have two categories, shading into one another yet distinguishable, both of which the Greeks called 'things which are (the case) by convention' (*nomōi*). These are:

(*a*) things which are in fact F, but are so only because people have decided that they should be regarded as being F.

(*b*) things which are not in fact F, but are merely called F. In so far as it is disputable how far anything actually becomes F by being generally regarded as, or generally said to be F, these two categories and hence the two distinctions shade into one another. In the present instance, sense (*a*) seems to be more clearly indicated; Hippias is not saying that the artificial political divisions between the various Greek states do not exist at all, but rather that while they do indeed exist and have undoubted force, they exist only because people have decided that they should. In this passage, as in most other instances, we find a devaluation of the conventional in favour of the real or natural; this is most marked in moral contexts, where the contrast is used to devalue conventional morality in favour of some supposedly more natural (i.e. higher) morality, frequently a 'morality' of unrestricted self-indulgence and self-aggrandizement, as in the most notorious instances, the speech of Callicles in the *Gorgias* (482c–486c, esp. 482c–484c) and a papyrus fragment of the sophist Antiphon (DK 87 B 44), but sometimes a more enlightened humanitarianism, e.g. Ar. *Pol.* 1. 3, 1253^{b}20–3: 'Others affirm that the rule of a master over slaves is contrary to nature, and that the distinction between slave and free man exists by convention only, and not by nature; and being an interference with nature is therefore unjust.' It was one of Plato's main concerns to show that in the area of morality the contrast does not exist, in that the demands of conventional morality, especially justice and *sōphrosunē*, arise naturally from the conditions of human life. Protagoras maintains the same position in this dialogue.

338e–339a In view of Protagoras' general educational programme, and in view of his comments on the poem, it seems likely that he saw the importance of literary criticism rather in developing the critical faculty and the exact use of language than in promoting the understanding and appreciation of poetry as an end in itself.

Simonides (*c.*556–468) was one of the most celebrated lyric poets. The poem quoted here was probably written when he was living in Thessaly (in northern Greece) as the guest of one of the aristocratic families of the region, the Scopads, one of whom, Scopas son of Creon, is mentioned at 339a7. It survives only in the quotations given here.

339c Pittacus was ruler of Mytilene on the island of Lesbos, at the end of the seventh century, and was reckoned as one of the Seven Sages (see Explanatory Note on 343a–b).

339e *a fellow citizen*: Simonides came, like Prodicus, from Ceos.

340a *Iliad* 21. 308–9.

340d A paraphrase of *Works and Days* 289, 291–2.

341e *never a Cean*: the Ceans had a reputation for uprightness.

342a While Socrates' references to philosophy in Crete and Sparta are of course ironical (for Spartan attitudes to intellectual matters see e.g. *Hipp. Maj.* 285b–e), admiration for the institutions and particularly for the educational systems of the two states was shared by many Greeks, including Plato. See *Rep.* 8. 544c, *Hipp. Maj.* 283e–284b, *Laws passim*, e.g. 1. 631b, 636e; cf. Ar. *EN* 1. 13, 1102^{a}7–11.

342b *wise men*: lit. 'sophists'. Also in 342c5 and 7.

343a–b The Greeks traditionally recognized a list of seven wise men, mostly historical persons of the seventh and sixth centuries, to which this is the earliest surviving reference. While there was some variation in the list (see D.L. 1. 13 and 40–2 (the latter passage in DK 10.1)), they were always seven in number. They were renowned chiefly as lawgivers and founts of practical wisdom, expressed in a number of maxims, of which the most famous were the two quoted here.

343b *Laconian*: i.e. Spartan. Laconia was the district surrounding the city of Sparta. 'Laconic' is derived from the name.

345d–e Socrates' claim that his thesis is universally accepted by the wise is ironical, as it was generally regarded as outrageously implausible (e.g. *Gorg.* 475e, Ar. *EN* 7. 2, 1145^{b}25–8).

The poem deals with a number of themes which were current in the poetry of the sixth and fifth centuries, such as the impossibility of perfection, the unbridgeable gulf between gods and men, the ineluctable vicissitudes of human life, and the necessity for moderation in everything. In representing Socrates as wrenching the poem from this historical context in order to interpret it in the light of his own, quite different, interests, Plato presumably intends to point out a fault in the methods of interpretation which he judged characteristic of the sophists. We have no means of estimating the extent to which this implied criticism was justified.

347c–e It is to be assumed that Plato intends the interpretation which Socrates has just given to show in an exemplary fashion what he regards as the cardinal fault in literary interpretation, namely the impossibility of definitively establishing the writer's meaning, with its consequent licence to factitious 'interpretations'. While Plato may perhaps have thought that this was particularly true of poetry (cf. *Hipp. Min.* 365c–d), he also held that in general the written word could not impart true knowledge, since knowledge implies an ability to formulate and defend one's views which requires that they be inculcated and tested by the method of question and answer (see *Phaedr.* 274b–277a, *Ep.* 7. 341c–d). See Introduction.

Frede *RM* 1985–6 takes the reference to the decorous dinner-party as a reference to Plato's *Symposium*, a hypothesis which she supports by the observation that, apart from Aristophanes, all the characters of the *Symposium* are present in the *Protagoras*, though only Socrates and Alcibiades speak. In order to reconcile this hypothesis with her assumed early dating of the *Protagoras* she posits a revision of the original discussion of the poem in the light of the doctrine of *Symp.* 207e that knowledge (contrary to *Meno* 97d) is not necessarily a stable possession.

This strikes me as ingenious but contrived. I suspect that the overlap with the dramatis personae of the *Symposium* is rather to be explained by the fact that many of the characters mentioned as listening to the sophists, including most of those who appear in the *Symposium*, later went to the bad in one way or another. Phaedrus, Eryximachus, and Alcibiades were involved in the profanation of the mysteries, as was Adeimantus. Three others mentioned as present, Charmides, Critias, and Andron, were active in anti-democratic movements. Agathon later left Athens to take up residence at the court of Archelaus of Macedon, who is mentioned in the *Gorgias* (470–1) as the paradigm of the wicked tyrant. Perhaps Plato intends to suggest that these were all people whose subsequent careers showed how, like Hippocrates, they risked their souls by associating with the sophists.

348d *Iliad* 10. 224–5.

349e–350c For discussion of this argument see Taylor, *Protagoras* comm.

351b–362a This section, which is the argumentative core of the dialogue, is a continuous passage of argument, raising many issues which are both individually complex and interrelated in complex ways. As such, it does not lend itself to useful treatment in the form of explanatory notes. See Introduction, and for fuller discussion Taylor, *Protagoras* comm.

INDEX

A. *Passages of ancient works cited (excluding the Protagoras)*

Ameipsias:
  Konnos general: 72
Antiphon:
  DK 87 B 44: 82
Aristophanes:
  Clouds general: 67, 71, 72
  Thesmophoriazusae general: 73
Aristotle:
  EN 1.13, 1102a7–11: 83
    3.10: 79
    7.2, 1145b25–8: 84
  Met. M4, 1978b27–9: 72
  Poetics 1447b9–13: xiii
  Pol. 1.3, 1253b20–3: 82

Critias:
  DK 88: 69

Diogenes Laertius:
  1.13: 83
  1.40–2: 83
  2.40: 70
  9.52: 81
  9.55: 75

Eupolis
  Flatterers general: 72, 74

Herodotus:
  6.105.1: 81
Hesiod:
  Works and Days 289, 291–2: 83
Homer:
  Iliad 10.224–5: 85
    21.308–9: 83
  Odyssey 10.494–5: 72

Pherecrates:
  Savages general: 78

Plato:
  Alc. I general: 68
    103a–104d: 70
    118e: 75
  Alc. II general: 68
  Apol. general: ix, xxiii
    19e: 67, 68
    33a–b: 70
  Charm. general: 69, 72, 80
    155c–e: 70
    163b–d: 82
    171d–176a: 80
  Crit. 110–12: 75
  Crito general: xxii, xxiii
    47d–48a: xxiii
  Euthyd. 277e–278a: 82
  Gorg. general: xxii, xxiii
    470–1: 85
    475e: 84
    481d: 70
    482c–486c (esp. 482c–484c): 82
    487c: 73
    491d: 79
    521d: 72
  Hipp. Maj. general: 68
    282e: 67
    283e–284b: 83
    285b–e: 83
  Hipp. Min. general: 68
    363c–364a: 81
    365c–d: 84
  Lach. 197b–d: 82
  Laws general: 83
    631b: 83
    636c: 83
    676–82: 75
  Meno general: xv, xxii–xxiii
    71b: xv

B. *General index*

Figures in **bold type** refer to the text of the dialogue.

INDEX

Kahn, C. H.: xxiii, 75
Kerferd, G. B.: 71, 75
knowledge (= *epistēmē*):
   344c–345b, 350a–351a,
   351b–d, 357a–e, 361b–c;
   xvi, xix–xx

laws (= *nomoi*, also
   conventions): 326d–e,
   327c–d
Lenaea: 327d; 78
Lesbos: 341c; 83
like (= *hoios*): 330a–331d; 78–9
Lombardo, S.: 79
lust, sexual desire (= *erōs*): 352b;
   70

Marathon: 81
measurement (= *metrētikē*
   (sc. *technē*)): 356c–357d
Megara: 316e
Mende: 315a; 72
Musaeus: 316d
Myrrinus: 315c; 73
Myson, *see* Seven Sages
Mytilene: 83

nature (= *phusis*): 323c–d,
   337c–d, 351a–b, 358d
opp. convention: 337c–d; xi,
   82–3

Odysseus: 72
Olympic Games: 81
opposite (= *enantion*): 331d,
   332a–333b, 360c–d
Orpheus: 315b, 316d
Orthagoras: 318c; 74

pain, distress (= *lupē* and *ania*),
   painful, unpleasant
   (= *lupēros* and *aniaros*):
   351b–e, 352a–357e
Paralus, son of Pericles: 315a,
   328c
Pausanias: 315d; 73
Peloponnesian War: 70, 72, 73

Penner, T.: xix, xx
Pericles: 315a, 319e–320a, 329a;
   72, 75
Phaedrus: 315c; 73, 85
Pheidias: 311c–e; 71
Pheidippides: 81
Philippides: 315a; 72
Phrynondas: 327d; 78
Pittacus: 339e–347a; xvii, 83
Plato *passim*
pleasure (= *hēdonē* and *to hēdu*),
   pleasant (= *hēdus*): 337c,
   351b–e, 352a–357e,
   358a–360e; *see* hedonism
Plutarch: 75
poetry, criticism of: 338e–348a;
   xvi–xix, 83, 84
Polycleitus: 311c, 328c; 71
Polycrates: 70
power (= *dunamis*): 330a–b,
   331d, 333a
praiseworthy, fine fair (= *kalos*),
   see beautiful
Prodicus: 314c, 315c–316a,
   317c–e, 336d, 337a–c,
   339e–341e, 342a, 357e,
   358a–b, 358d–e, 359a; xvii,
   68, 81–2, 83
Prometheus: 320d–322a, 361d; xv
Protagoras *passim*
Protagorean subjectivism: 67,
   76–7, 81
punishment: 323c–324d,
   325a–d, 326d–e; 77–8

relativism: 81
result (= *telos*): 354b–d

Scamander: 340a
Scopas: 339a; 83
self-predication: 79
Selymbria: 316e; 73
Seven Sages: 343a; xvii, 83
sex, *see* lust
shameful, disgraceful, foul
   (= *aischros*), *see* ugly
Simoeis: 340a

91

The Oxford World's Classics Website

www.worldsclassics.co.uk

- Browse the full range of Oxford World's Classics online
- Sign up for our monthly e-alert to receive information on new titles
- Read extracts from the Introductions
- Listen to our editors and translators talk about the world's greatest literature with our Oxford World's Classics audio guides
- Join the conversation, follow us on Twitter at OWC_Oxford
- Teachers and lecturers can order inspection copies quickly and simply via our website

www.worldsclassics.co.uk

American Literature

British and Irish Literature

Children's Literature

Classics and Ancient Literature

Colonial Literature

Eastern Literature

European Literature

Gothic Literature

History

Medieval Literature

Oxford English Drama

Poetry

Philosophy

Politics

Religion

The Oxford Shakespeare

A complete list of Oxford World's Classics, including Authors in Context, Oxford English Drama, and the Oxford Shakespeare, is available in the UK from the Marketing Services Department, Oxford University Press, Great Clarendon Street, Oxford OX2 6DP, or visit the website at www.oup.com/uk/worldsclassics.

In the USA, visit www.oup.com/us/owc for a complete title list.

Oxford World's Classics are available from all good bookshops. In case of difficulty, customers in the UK should contact Oxford University Press Bookshop, 116 High Street, Oxford OX1 4BR.

	Classical Literary Criticism
	The First Philosophers: The Presocrates and the Sophists
	Greek Lyric Poetry
	Myths from Mesopotamia
APOLLODORUS	The Library of Greek Mythology
APOLLONIUS OF RHODES	Jason and the Golden Fleece
APULEIUS	The Golden Ass
ARISTOPHANES	Birds and Other Plays
ARISTOTLE	The Nicomachean Ethics
	Physics
	Politics
BOETHIUS	The Consolation of Philosophy
CAESAR	The Civil War
	The Gallic War
CATULLUS	The Poems of Catullus
CICERO	Defence Speeches
	The Nature of the Gods
	On Obligations
	The Republic and The Laws
EURIPIDES	Bacchae and Other Plays
	Medea and Other Plays
	Orestes and Other Plays
	The Trojan Women and Other Plays
GALEN	Selected Works
HERODOTUS	The Histories
HOMER	The Iliad
	The Odyssey